This Book Belongs To

THE BOOK OF KINGS

Magnificent MONARCHS, Notorious NOBLES, and DISTINGUISHED DUDES Who Ruled THE WORLD

CALEB MAGYAR AND
STEPHANIE WARREN DRIMMER

NATIONAL GEOGRAPHIC
WASHINGTON, D.C.

CONTENTS

William III,
Revolutionary
Ruler

ALL HAIL THE KING! 6

CHAPTER ONE

EMPIRE BUILDERS 8
Hammurabi 10
Self-Made Monarchs.................. 12
The Unifiers 14
Stop-at-Nothing Nobles 16
King Kamehameha 18
Pachacuti Inca Yupanqui............ 20
Beyond Borders 22
Church & State..................... 24
Bow Down to the Crown!............ 26

CHAPTER TWO

**MILITARY
MASTERMINDS**.. 28
Genghis Khan....... 30
Viking Kings........ 32
Crusader Kings....... 34
Turf Wars 36
The Art of War 38
Shaka 40
Repressing Revolt........ 42
Daring Defenders....... 44
Formidable
Fortresses 46

CHAPTER THREE

RULERS IN REVOLUTION 48
William III......................... 50
Et Tu, Buddy?...................... 52
Of Might and Mercy 54
Comeback Kings 56
Revolution in the Philippines........ 58
Simón Bolívar 60
Facing Defeat 62
Men of the People 64
In Shining Armor 66

CHAPTER FOUR

LORDS OF LEGEND 68
Gilgamesh........................... 70
Founding Figures 72
Kingly Characters........ 74
Kings of the Gods 76
Legendary Swords 78
Minos................. 80
Mythical Monarchs..... 82
Kings of Mischief 84
Godly Gadgets........ 86

Genghis Khan,
Conquering
King

Aragorn,
Legendary
Leader

Richard I,
Crusader King

Lin Manuel-Miranda, Monarch of Music (left);
3D Printing, Noble Technology of Tomorrow (below)

CHAPTER SEVEN

CHAPTER FIVE

KINGS OF CREATIVITY 88
Lin-Manuel Miranda 90
Kings of the Console 92
Sovereigns of Sound 94
Rulers of Rhythm and Rhyme 96
The Teenagers Who Invented Superman 98
Frank Gehry 100
Visionary Masters 102
Movie Monarchs 104
And the Oscar Goes to 106

KINGS OF CHANGE 128
Jadav Payeng 130
Noble Nobels 132
Monarchs of Morality 134
Celebrities Worth Celebrating 136
3D Printing 138
Louis Braille 140
Kings of Tomorrow 142
Kings of Hearts 144
Strength in Numbers 146

CHAPTER EIGHT

CHAPTER SIX

KINGS OF KNOWLEDGE 148
Isaac Newton 150
Science's Dynamic Duos 152
Computer Kings 154
Emperors of Exploration 156
Moon Walkers 158
    Carl Sagan 160
    Monarchs of the Great Outdoors 162
    Dinosaur Kings 164
    Dare to Explore 166

Your Turn to Wear the Crown . . 168
Index 170
Photo Credits 175
Acknowledgments . . . 176

ARISTOCRATS OF ACTION . . . 108
Babe Ruth 110
Kings of the Silver Screen 112
Kings of Combat 114
Game Changers 116
Noble Up-and-Comers 118
George Williams 120
Rulers of Their Game 122
Kings of Climbing 124
Ruler of the Ring 126

Jimmy Chin,
King of the Climb

Moon Walkers, Lords
of the Lunar Surface

ALL HAIL THE KING!

Haïle Selassie I,
Emperor of Ethiopia

Power and might. Since the beginning of human history, people have tried to attain these things—and many succeeded. Whether they were called kings, emperors, sultans, khans, or czars, for thousands of years men have stepped forward to lead others through peaceful periods and turbulent times. Many were beloved by their people, hailed as promoters of progress and saints of civility, while others were despised for their brutality and ruthlessness. Some came to power using their brains; others used their brawn to achieve royal status, pushing aside all foes that stood in their way. But one thing they all share is that years, or in some cases centuries, later, we're still reading and learning about these individuals and their incredible feats.

Simón Bolívar, Hero of a Revolution

You may have heard of some of them, like King Henry VIII, made famous by movies and popular culture. Others, like Ethiopian emperor Haile Selassie, you might be reading about for the first time. From Babylonian king Hammurabi, whose famous code of justice ultimately helped shape today's United States judicial system, to conqueror Genghis Khan, who created the largest empire the world has ever seen, these are men from around the globe who shaped the history of their nations—and of the world.

Kings of a Different Kind
Not all kings wield scepters or sit on fancy thrones. Within these pages, you'll also find stand-out innovators and leaders. These are people like Dr. Martin Luther King, Jr., who championed the rights of African Americans during the U.S. civil rights movement, and revolutionary renegade Simón Bolívar. Courageous changemakers also lead in many different ways— whether as illustrious inventors,

Martin Luther King, Jr., Civil Rights Leader

sports superstars, or titans of technology. Others have special talents for storytelling or saving wildlife. These men may never have worn jewel-encrusted crowns, but they certainly made their mark.

Getting Real About Royals
One thing to remember as you read is that history isn't always pretty. People are human, capable of good and bad, and while many of these monarchs did great things, some did just the opposite. But whether royal or not, all of these men have left behind lessons we can learn from.

These pages tell the tale of our human story and how these daring dudes helped make our world into what it is today. By the end of this book, you might be wondering why you've never heard of some of these legendary leaders and their audacious actions. From kings and commanders to protesters and peacemakers to artists and astronauts, get ready to dig in to the lives of some of the world's most influential men.

LeBron James, King of the Court

As you read *The Book of Kings*, keep an eye out for these royal extras:

COMMANDING QUEENS
This book is mostly about fearless fellows—but that doesn't mean there's no room for powerful women! These sidebars showcase some of history's most legendary leading ladies. To learn more about fascinating female rulers, pick up *The Book of Queens*.

FIT FOR A KING
Each chapter ends with a closer look into the world of kings, from their clothing to their castles to their compatriots.

EMPIRE BUILDERS

Every king has a story about how he came to wear the crown. Some were born into royalty, some married into it, and a few simply declared themselves top dog of a brand-new kingdom. But claiming the throne is one thing; keeping it is another. To go down in history, most monarchs had to be smart and savvy, knowing when to negotiate for peace and when it was time to show their dominance on the battlefield. The kings in these pages rose to power to become some of history's greatest empire builders—and rulers to remember.

A statue of Pachacuti
Inca Yupanqui stands
at Machu Picchu, Peru.

HAMMURABI

⚔ KING OF JUSTICE ⚔

Hammurabi became the king of the Mesopotamian city-state of Babylon when he was just 18. But he didn't let his youth and lack of experience stop him from making a big impression. This king kept the peace among his people while conquering many other cities and lands, eventually extending his control throughout Mesopotamia.

LIVING UP TO A LEGACY

When he inherited Babylon from his father, Hammurabi had a lot to live up to. His father—known as Sin-Muballit—was very popular with his subjects. According to his own records, Sin-Muballit successfully fought off invaders and strengthened his city's defenses. He also oversaw the building of irrigation ditches to improve farming, which helped keep his people well fed and happy.

When Hammurabi came to power in 1795 B.C., he wasted no time picking up where his father had left off. He continued improving the irrigation system and fortifying Babylon's stone walls to protect his people. He also built many temples, including one to Marduk, the patron deity of the city, to give his subjects a place to worship. Perhaps his boldest move was forgiving all private debts among his people. That was a big deal to the Babylonians, since being indebted in ancient Mesopotamia meant you could be enslaved. Unsurprisingly, the people loved their new king.

It is believed that the name Hammurabi meant "the kinsman is a healer."

IT'S WAR

Life was good in Babylon. But beyond its boundaries, trouble lurked. Several surrounding city-states wanted control of the Tigris and Euphrates Rivers, and Hammurabi's kingdom just so happened to sit right between them.

ROYAL RUNDOWN

➤ **BORN:** 1810 B.C., Babylon ➤ **DIED:** 1750 B.C., Babylon ➤ **LED:** Babylon
➤ **REMEMBERED FOR:** The Code of Hammurabi and improving his subjects' quality of life

One city-state, Elam, was on the warpath: After conquering a couple of neighboring cities, it set its sights on Babylon. But Hammurabi thought quickly and reached out to an ally, Rim-Sin, the king of the town of Larsa, just downriver from Babylon. The kingdoms combined forces and, together, crushed the Elamites.

The battle was won—but Hammurabi was too smart to sit back and celebrate. He knew he'd next have to conquer Larsa to continue to reign over the rivers—and to protect his kingdom for the long run. So, with their common foe out of the picture, Hammurabi turned against his former ally.

RIDING THE WAVE

It didn't really seem like Babylon could stand a chance against Larsa. Rim-Sin had more land, more men, and more weapons. But Hammurabi had one very powerful tool in his possession: the Euphrates River. He ordered the river be dammed to cut off water to his enemy downstream. He then destroyed the dam, unleashing a giant wall of water that slammed Larsa, leaving it reeling. Their enemy weakened, the armies of Babylon swooped in to capture their rival.

With this stunning victory behind him, Hammurabi became hungry for more power. He continued to capture the cities of Mesopotamia, eventually elevating Babylon's status to the most powerful city in the region. By 1750 B.C., Hammurabi had grown Babylon from a handful of small cities to an empire that covered all of ancient Mesopotamia.

But despite his success on the battlefield, Hammurabi is not remembered as an empire builder. Instead, he's best known for his focus on improving the lives of his people. His sense of justice even extended to those he conquered: Hammurabi provided the people of his captured cities the same privileges he granted his own, such as forgiving their debts, building walls, and making repairs to their cities. And most famously, Hammurabi is remembered as the writer of the Code of Hammurabi, a list of laws, fines, and punishments that is one of the oldest legal codes in the world.

CRACKING HAMMURABI'S CODE

Hammurabi was a stickler for justice. He carved his long list of rules and regulations—282 in total—onto a massive pillar of black stone for all his people to see. The code covered everything from a doctor's fee (10 silver shekels for a gentleman, two for a slave) to the punishment for stealing an ox (the thief had to pay back up to 30 times the animal's value). Included in the code are some edicts that form the foundation of the modern legal system, such as the principle that those accused of crimes are considered innocent until proven guilty. And Hammurabi's law of retaliation, often called "an eye for an eye," is mostly used as a metaphor today—but in his kingdom, it literally meant that when someone was found guilty of hurting another person, he would be punished by having the same painful act inflicted on him. Hammurabi's code was so influential that the U.S. Supreme Court building features a marble carving of the king—to this day, the ancient leader still keeps watch over the judicial system his code helped to create.

SELF-MADE
MONARCHS

Crowning Themselves King

Sometimes the quickest way to become king is simply to create your own kingdom. These inventive monarchs made bold moves to turn fledgling lands into their own powerful provinces.

SPECIAL SON:
Stephen I of Hungary (ca A.D. 975–1038)

Before Stephen was born, Hungary had no kings or organized religion. Instead, Stephen's ancestors—a tribe of nomadic raiders—were loosely ruled by chieftains and grand princes. As a result, the Hungarians had little power in Europe. That all changed when Stephen's father, Géza, had him baptized as a Catholic, hoping his son could forge alliances with other European kings if they shared the same religion. The plan paid off when Stephen married the sister of the most powerful monarch in Europe, the Holy Roman emperor. The marriage catapulted Stephen to a new level of power, and he eventually declared himself the first king of Hungary. He established religion throughout the country, strengthening Christianity through decrees and laws—even making the building of churches mandatory. Today, Stephen I is celebrated as the patron saint of Hungary.

THE FIRST KING OF PORTUGAL:
Afonso I (ca A.D. 1109–1185)

Afonso, sometimes called Afonso Henriques, was about three years old when his father, the Count of Portugal, died. Because Afonso was much too young to govern the country, then part of the kingdom of Galicia, his mother, Teresa de León, ruled in his place. During that time, she plotted to stay in power even after her son became old enough to rule. But when Afonso grew up, he wanted to claim his crown for himself. He rallied an army and first defeated his mother's troops, then captured her. He stripped her of her power and began to conquer much of what is modern-day Portugal. In 1129, he declared himself king of the region, and in 1143, won Portugal's independence from the medieval Spanish kingdom León.

THE FIRST KING OF ALL ENGLAND:
Æthelstan (ca A.D. 895–939)

There were plenty of kings *in* England, but there had never been a king of *all* England until Æthelstan (ETH-el-stan). He was crowned king of the Mercians, one of the ancient Anglo-Saxon kingdoms that once made up what is now called England, in A.D. 924. Right away, Æthelstan exhibited strong leadership qualities and smart battle sense. He went up against rulers of surrounding territories, including the notorious Vikings, and conquered one after another. Some historical sources say he never lost a battle, and his stellar record eventually earned him the nickname "Æthelstan the Glorious." He even got the five kings of Wales to pay him gold, silver, and 25,000 oxen each year. In 937, Æthelstan defeated an invasion of the Scots, Welsh, and Danes and became the first king to rule all of England. Though he was fierce on the battlefield, he was also known for generosity toward his subjects, as well as his patronage of education and religious institutions.

THE CONNECTOR:
Narmer of Egypt (ca 3150 B.C.–3088 B.C.)

There's not much in the history books about the life of Narmer—after all, he lived so long ago that his reign predated all but the very first hieroglyphic carvings. But some historians believe he is responsible for one very important historical event: uniting Egypt into a single, peaceful kingdom. Prior to Narmer coming into power some 5,000 years ago, the empire was split in two, Upper and Lower Egypt. It's said that Narmer, who already ruled Upper Egypt, took control of Lower Egypt in battle. He then combined the groups and became the first king to lead all of Egypt. At the time, Narmer's kingdom was the world's largest land area ruled by a single person.

COMMANDING QUEENS

GODDESS QUEEN
Dido of Carthage
(ca 800s B.C.)

Famous for founding Carthage, a city in modern-day Tunisia, Africa, this queen's rise to the top is nothing short of legendary. Some historians think Dido's story is based on historical fact, but others think she was a totally fictional figure. Ancient writers tell a tale of a runaway princess who escaped her hometown after her brother threatened to kill her so that he could become king. As she traveled, Dido gained a large following, and by the time she reached North Africa, she decided to settle with them and built a new city on a hill, which she named Carthage. There, she ruled as queen and became so beloved that after she died, the people of Carthage worshipped her as a goddess.

HIAWATHA

⊷ HEARTBROKEN HERO ⊷

Thousands of years ago, Native Americans settled on the banks of the Great Lakes and the St. Lawrence River in what is now New York State, U.S.A., and Ontario, Canada. Although these settlers represented different tribes (Onondaga, Mohawk, Oneida, Cayuga, and Seneca), they were all part of the Iroquois nation. They shared similar cultures and spoke the same language, yet they were constantly at war with one another. And their bitter battles were weakening the nation.

Onondaga leader Hiawatha experienced this violence firsthand when, according to legend, five of his daughters were killed by enemies. Heartbroken, the chief sought out a spiritual leader named Deganawida, also known as the Great Peacemaker. The story goes that Deganawida encouraged Hiawatha to forgive his enemies and focus on embracing peace. His wise words healed Hiawatha of his sadness. In turn, the chief became determined to spread the prophet's message of peace throughout his nation.

Hiawatha wasted no time getting the word out. Despite the extreme danger of walking among enemies, he went from tribe to tribe to discuss the importance of putting aside their differences for the sake of the greater good. With Deganawida's principles of understanding and forgiveness to back him up, Hiawatha was a persuasive speaker, and people listened. He ultimately organized the Iroquois Confederacy, with the group agreeing to stand together against invasion while abiding by the standards of "peace, civil authority, righteousness, and the great law."

United by their national hero and the new constitution, the Iroquois Confederacy enjoyed a long-lasting peace, eventually becoming one of the strongest forces in northeastern North America during the 17th and 18th centuries.

> The framers of the U.S. Constitution were influenced by the principles of the Iroquois Confederacy, including peace and justice.

ROYAL RUNDOWN

➤ **LIVED:** ca 1450   ➤ **LED:** Iroquois Confederacy
➤ **REMEMBERED FOR:** Forming the Iroquois Confederacy

GAJAH MADA

⚔ ISLAND CONQUEROR ⚔

From peasant to prime minister, Gajah Mada's meteoric rise to the top was aided by his smarts, bravery, and loyalty.

Gajah Mada served as a bodyguard tasked with protecting King Jayanagara of the Majapahit Empire. When a rebel general named Kuti attempted to overthrow the king, Gajah Mada managed to whisk the monarch away to a hiding spot. He then spread a rumor that the king had been killed. By observing who seemed upset and who seemed happy with this misinformation, Gajah Mada was able to discover who the king's supporters really were.

Gajah Mada secretly organized a revolt against Kuti and helped to restore the rightful king to the throne. For his loyalty, King Jayanagara made his faithful subject his prime minister. Though Gajah Mada never became royalty, he became the power behind the throne, doing much of the ruling himself. As prime minister, Gajah Mada made his main mission expanding his land. To prove just how serious he was, he took an oath, called the Sumpah Palapa, in which he denied himself any food made with spices until he had conquered all of the islands surrounding the Majapahit.

As it turned out, Gajah Mada had to avoid spiced dishes for 28 years. During that time, he built a powerful navy to spread the power and influence of Majapahit throughout the archipelago (as well as Singapore, Malaysia, Brunei, and the southern Philippines). In the end, Gajah Mada had successfully brought the entire region under the control of his empire. His influence continues to extend over much of modern-day Indonesia and Malaysia today: The first Indonesian university in Jogjakarta, founded in 1946, was named after him.

Gajah Mada was the first person to unite the territory that makes up modern Indonesia.

ROYAL RUNDOWN

➤→ **BORN:** 1290 ➤→ **DIED:** 1364 ➤→ **LED:** Majapahit Empire
➤→ **REMEMBERED FOR:** Unifying Indonesia

STOP-AT-NOTHING
NOBLES

Rulers Who Fought for the Right to Rule

History is full of leaders who had to battle their way to the top. Whether they clashed with fellow monarchs or feuded with family members, these kings refused to back down until they claimed the throne.

HEIR APPARENT: Shah Jahan (A.D. 1592–1666)

Wars of succession were common in northern India's Mogul Empire. When an emperor died, power was split among all his sons, who would then use political influence and military might to compete for the throne. To complicate matters further, the Mogul emperors often had multiple wives. Some of those wives wanted one of her sons to become emperor, so empresses often quietly plotted against each other's sons.

After leading an army that expanded the Mogul Empire in central India, Shah Jahan, the third son of Emperor Jahangir, was the clear favorite to inherit the throne. But the empress Nur Jahan tried to make her own son, Shah Jahan's youngest half brother, the heir by gathering supporters and fighters. When the emperor died, the brothers went to war. Shah Jahan won quickly, becoming emperor in 1628. He immediately arrested his stepmother and had his half brother executed. Shah Jahan was ruthless. However, he is best remembered for building the world-famous Taj Mahal as a tomb for his wife Mumtaz Mahal, a testament of his eternal love for her.

STUBBORN SOVEREIGN:
William the Conqueror (A.D. 1028–1087)

William had to learn to be strong from a young age. When his father, the Duke of Normandy, died suddenly, the nobles had no interest in being ruled by William. They were constantly rebelling and even killed off the young duke's guardians in an attempt to overthrow him. That experience helped shape William into the ruthless ruler he was to become.

In 1051, William visited his cousin Edward I, the king of England. According to Norman legend, Edward promised the crown to William. So imagine William's surprise when Edward died and another loyal subject, Earl Harold Godwinson, was named king instead. Enraged at the deception and

ORIGINAL EMPEROR: Octavian (63 B.C.–A.D. 14)

The journey Octavian (also known as Caesar Augustus) took before becoming the first emperor of Rome was a rocky one. The nephew of the great Roman dictator Julius Caesar, Octavian learned that he was in line to the throne after his uncle was assassinated in 44 B.C. Octavian was eager to take over, but he had to sidestep a few enemies before he could wear the crown: The same assassins who had slayed Caesar were after his heir, too. Octavian rallied two of Julius Caesar's biggest supporters—Mark Antony and Marcus Lepidus—to successfully help him track down the killers and avenge the dictator's death.

Octavian wasn't in the clear just yet, though. Mark Antony and his new wife, Egyptian queen Cleopatra, were angling to take charge of Rome themselves. Octavian battled their army, ultimately defeating them. After that, there was no one left to oppose Octavian, and he was named the first emperor of Rome.

RELENTLESS WARRIOR:
Oda Nobunaga (A.D. 1534–1582)

Unwilling to give up his titles and the lands he had inherited from his father, 16th-century Japanese ruler Oda Nobunaga held strong against a much more powerful monarch—and his army. It all started when Nobunaga's father, Oda Nobuhide, died in 1551. Nobunaga readied to take on the job he'd been preparing for his entire life: as a minor *daimyo*—or feudal ruler—in the province of Owari, on Japan's biggest island.

But first he had to defeat Imagawa Yoshimoto, a leader of a nearby land who wanted to take control of Owari. It was no easy task: Yoshimoto was a tough challenger with a huge and powerful army. But luck was on Nobunaga's side: One night, as his men gathered in the woods near Yoshimoto's war camp, a surprise thunderstorm blew in and masked their approach. Under the cover of the stormy night, Nobunaga's men surprised the enemy, killed Yoshimoto, and took charge of Owari. With that victory under his belt, Nobunaga next dreamed of conquest himself. He embraced a new weapon that had been brought to Japan by Portuguese traders in 1543: the musket, or long-barreled gun. During his military career, Nobunaga conquered much of central Japan by effectively using his firearm skills in battle.

determined to win the crown he was promised, William the Norman sailed to England with approximately 7,000 French fighting men. His army was able to land unchallenged because Harold was busy fighting in the Norwegian sea—against the Vikings. Harold then had to face William with an exhausted army in the Battle of Hastings. Harold was killed in that battle, and the throne went to William the Norman, today known as William the Conqueror.

This drawing shows William's castle, called Old Sarum, which he built inside a fortress once used by the Romans.

KING KAMEHAMEHA

THE FIRST RULER OF THE KINGDOM OF HAWAII

In this artist's depiction, King Kamehameha casts a lock of his hair into the crater of the Hualālai volcano to invoke Pele, the goddess of fire and volcanoes.

ROYAL RUNDOWN

➨ **BORN:** 1758 ➨ **DIED:** 1819 ➨ **LED:** Hawaii
➨ **REMEMBERED FOR:** Uniting Hawaii

According to ancient Hawaiian legend, a great chief would be born beneath the arrival of a huge, blazing bird who'd light up the night sky. Fittingly, legend says King Kamehameha made his grand entrance on Earth just as Halley's comet—with its feathery, birdlike tail—soared across the skies sometime around 1758. Whether that story is true or a tall tale, what's known is that Kamehameha was born into a royal family and eventually fit the bill of powerful chief, becoming the first king to unite all the Hawaiian islands.

THE LONELY ONE

Kamehameha, born with the name Pai'ea, spent his early childhood mostly alone and hidden away in secluded Waipi'o Valley. It was a solitary beginning for the kid who would be king, but Kamehameha's family was just making sure that no one from rival clans—who threatened the life of the young prince—could find him. Once the danger passed, the then five-year-old returned to his family in Kailua, who switched his name from Pai'ea to Kamehameha, meaning "the Lonely One."

STRONG SHOWING

Kamehameha, who was estimated to have been more than seven feet (2.1 m) tall, showed great strength even as a child. According to one famous story, he turned heads after picking up and flipping the monstrous Naha Stone, which was said to weigh between two and three tons (1.8 and 2.7 t). So it's no surprise that Kamehameha was selected to become *koa*, or a Hawaiian warrior, at an early age. He went to *pā lua*, a special school where he learned things like hand-to-hand combat and how to use weapons like spears and the *leiomano*, a wooden club lined with tiger shark teeth.

THE MAKING OF A WARRIOR

As koa, Kamehameha played a major role in a milestone in Hawaii's history. In 1779, British captain James Cook arrived on Hawaii for the third time. His first two visits—both part of Cook's explorations of the Pacific—had been peaceful. But a few days after finishing his second visit, Cook was forced to return to Hawaii due to bad weather. Cook and the Hawaiians clashed, and Cook kidnapped one of their chiefs. Cook's plan was quickly foiled, and the explorer was killed in the skirmish. Kamehameha's performance in the battle cemented his status as someone to respect, helping him on his way to become the first king of a united Hawaii.

LIKE UNCLE, LIKE NEPHEW

Aside from his formal schooling, Kamehameha received training from his uncle, King Kalaniʻōpuʻu, the ruler of the island of Hawaii. The king took his nephew under his wing and taught him skills in warfare, history, navigation, and religion... all things necessary to become a great chief. Kalaniʻōpuʻu didn't leave Kamehameha control over the island when he died, however; that title went to Kalaniʻōpuʻu's son instead, and the two cousins eventually fought for control.

A FIGHT TO THE TOP

It took many more years—and many battles—before Kamehameha came to rule Hawaii. First, he defeated his cousin Kiwalaʻo and then faced other foes on the islands, triumphing each time. By trading Hawaii's sandalwood for weapons from Western traders, Kamehameha racked up an impressive artillery for his army and eventually used that firepower to take charge of most of the Hawaiian islands. Finally, by 1810, Kamehameha had successfully united the islands and ruled as their high chief.

THE LAST QUEEN OF HAWAII
Liliuokalani (1838–1917)

COMMANDING QUEENS

Starting in 1820, colonists from the United States began moving to the island nation of Hawaii and taking control of its sugar plantations and trade. The first—and last—queen of Hawaii, Lȋliuokalani inherited the kingdom from her brother, Kalakaua, in 1891. Four years before, he had been forced by armed soldiers to sign a new constitution that stripped the Hawaiian monarchy of its power. As soon as she assumed the throne, Lȋliuokalani began working to reverse the unfair constitution forced on her people and to write a new one. But the new powers that controlled her nation wanted to stop her. Unable to stand up to the United States' superior military and unwilling to shed the blood of her people, Lȋliuokalani had no choice but to give up command of her nation. The United States overthrew the Hawaiian monarchy, and Hawaii became a U.S. territory. Lȋliuokalani's attempts to keep her country independent were unsuccessful, and she was even arrested and imprisoned. Still, she was beloved by the Hawaiian people. She lived out the end of her life as a private citizen and died at her home in Honolulu in 1917. Today, the last queen of Hawaii is celebrated as a symbol of Hawaiian culture and independence.

PACHACUTI INCA YUPANQUI

◆═══ EXPANDING THE INCA EMPIRE ═══►○

Pachacuti Yu Pan qui Decimo Ynga

Machu Picchu comprises more than 150 buildings. The structures are so well built that not even a knife blade can fit between their stones.

Nestled high in the Andes Mountains, the city of Cusco served as the capital and birthplace of the Inca Empire. There, in a lavish palace, lived the emperor, also known as the Sapa Inca ("the Only One"). Pachacuti Inca Yupanqui was the ninth Sapa Inca, and like those before him, he was the all-powerful leader of his people. The Inca believed that their kings had descended from the sun god, so they treated the Sapa Inca like a living deity. He sported huge gold earrings and clothes dripping with jewels and gold—and he never wore an outfit more than once! According to legend, the Sapa Inca's clothes were burned after just one wear.

GAME CHANGER

Pachacuti Inca Yupanqui—whose given name was Cusi—stands out among all the Sapa Inca because of how he forever changed the landscape of the kingdom of Cusco. But his rise to prominence and power wasn't a given. In fact, his father, Viracocha Inca, had actually named Cusi's older brother as the heir to the city of Cusco. Then, one day in the early 15th century, a neighboring rival known as the Chanca attacked Cusco. Cusi's father and brother fled to a mountain outpost, leaving their kingdom undefended. Cusi knew it was up to him to save the kingdom, so he

ROYAL RUNDOWN

➤➤ **BORN:** 1438 ➤➤ **DIED:** 1471 ➤➤ **LED:** Inca Empire
➤➤ **REMEMBERED FOR:** Expanding the Inca Empire and the creation of Machu Picchu

sprang into action, gathering a few warriors and mounting a defense against the invading Chanca. Ultimately, he succeeded in driving the more powerful enemy out of the city.

THE EARTH SHAKER

After his heroic efforts against the Chanca, Cusi—who changed his name to Pachacuti, meaning "Earth Shaker"—took over as leader of Cusco. When he came to power, Cusco was still under constant enemy attack, so Pachacuti decided to go on the offensive. He built up his army and set off to take over Lake Titicaca. The Inca army conquered the native people who lived on the lake, bringing them under Pachacuti's rule. This conquest was a sign of things to come for Cusco, which would continue to grow and grow under Pachacuti's power.

THE INCA EMPIRE

Pachacuti eventually conquered so many territories that his empire became bigger than anything ever seen in the Americas at the time. To unify his kingdom, built roads winding down the Andes Mountains—not an easy feat on the steep slopes. These roads linked towns and sacred sites, making it easier for Cusco citizens to get around.

Pachacuti went down in history as an empire builder, but he was also a ruler ahead of his time. He set up a system of storage houses around his kingdom, stocked with excess supplies so that the people of Cusco would never go hungry during a drought or bad harvest. He also had historians record important events on painted tablets and created a calendar—all more than 3,000 years ago!

MAKING MACHU PICCHU

Pachacuti Inca Yupanqui was so powerful he literally moved mountains. Or, rather, he ordered enough rock and earth to be removed from the top of a mountain range until he had a flat area large enough to build a city of 1,000 people. That city? Machu Picchu, which historians believe Pachacuti built as either his fortress, a mountain retreat, or some sort of shrine. Whatever its purpose, Machu Picchu became one of the most sacred sites for the Inca, remaining this way even after Pachacuti's death, until it was abandoned after the Spanish conquistadores arrived in South America in the 1500s. Today, people from all over the world flock to the site, making the trip up miles of steep, winding roads to stand and marvel at the remains of the city, a testament to the tenacity of Pachacuti and his people.

BEYOND **BORDERS**

Turning Kingdoms Into Empires

How do you build an empire? To start, you need a strong leader who can merge multiple civilizations—and then keep control. Sometimes, the process is peaceful. Other times, leaders wield an iron fist to unite kingdoms in their grasp.

EFFICIENT EMPEROR:
Charlemagne (ca A.D. 742–ca A.D. 814)

Growing up, Charles carefully watched his father, King Pepin the Short, expand his kingdom's borders while supporting the pope, head of the Catholic Church in Rome. When Charles became king of the Franks, a group of Germanic-speaking people in western Europe, he followed in his father's footsteps. Charles expanded his borders west into Spain, south into Italy, and east past Germany. His mission was to unite his people under the common religion of Christianity. As his borders expanded, he became known as Charles the Great, or Charlemagne in the Frankish language. Then, in the year A.D. 800, Christianity's stronghold was rocked when rebels in Rome attempted to overthrow Pope Leo III. Charlemagne marched his armies south and saved the pope, and, in thanks, Pope Leo III declared Charlemagne emperor of the Romans. By the time he died in 814, Charlemagne controlled an empire that covered much of western Europe.

CAUTIOUS KING:
Qin Shi Huang Di (ca 259 B.C.–210 B.C.)

The unification of China came at a steep price for Qin Shi Huang Di. He had defeated the states of the Chu, Han, Wei, Yan, and Zhao; in 221 B.C. the last holdout, the kingdom of Qi, submitted to his rule, too. For the first time in history, northern China was a single empire. But Qin had made vicious enemies in each of the six kingdoms he had subdued. After surviving several assassination attempts, Qin tightened his grip on the other kingdoms. He expelled diplomats and ordered any book that wasn't about him and his triumphs to be burned. Qin was so concerned with his safety that he ordered the construction of a 3,000-to-4,000-mile (4,800-to-6,400-km)-long great wall that would keep invaders out. But not even that was enough for him. Qin still wanted to be protected *after* he died. So he was buried with a vast terra-cotta army, thousands of life-size clay soldiers to guard him in the afterlife.

FROM EXILE TO EMPIRE:
Sundiata Keita (ca 1235)

As a teenager, Sundiata Keita left his homeland, Manden, in what is now Mali, Africa. He was forced into exile as the younger half brother of the new monarch, Dankaran-Tuman. Sundiata's popularity and predicted powers had made Dankaran-Tuman jealous. Years later, Sundiata's homeland was attacked by a rival state while he dwelled in exile in the desert. Determined to regain his home and become king, Sundiata managed to form an army, defeat his rivals, and take back his land. And he didn't stop there: Sundiata sent his generals in all directions, bringing more and more kingdoms under his control. By 1255, near the end of his reign, the newly established empire of Mali stretched from the salt mines of the Sahara to the gold fields of the West African forests. As emperor, Sundiata left a glittering legacy: For generations, his empire provided much of the gold used to strike coins in the Middle East and Europe. His legendary story has even been turned into an epic poem which is still recited and studied today around the world.

KIND CONQUEROR:
Cyrus the Great (ca 580 B.C.–ca 529 B.C.)

Most emperors didn't give a second thought to the well-being of the people they conquered. Not much is known about his early life, but Cyrus was born around 580 B.C. in Persia, or modern-day Iran. As a young man, he took the throne of one of the region's many kingdoms. Now a commander, Cyrus began taking on entire kingdoms, and by 549, he had established an empire. Cyrus knew something that few conquerors before him did: He could never command a vast realm if he forced people in foreign kingdoms to give up their own customs. So instead, Cyrus allowed the people in his empire to keep their traditions and continue worshipping their own gods. This bold innovation in conquest made Cyrus one of the most successful emperors of the ancient world.

COMMANDING QUEENS

FIRST RULER OF JAPAN
Queen Himiko
(ca A.D. 3rd century)

When Queen Himiko came to power, Japan was made up of hundreds of individual nations scattered across the archipelago. It would take a powerful ruler to control not just one of these nations but to unify them into an empire. That person was Himiko, the first known ruler in Japanese history. Stories say that Himiko lived in a fortress guarded by 100 men, with 1,000 female attendants, and her people believed she was a sorceress with magical powers. Himiko didn't only unite Japan; she was also a masterful diplomat who sent ambassadors across 500 miles (805 km) of angry ocean just to offer a few gifts to the Wei emperor. Impressed by Himiko's thoughtfulness, the emperor sent back emissaries loaded with bronze mirrors and swords. Much of the story of Japan's first leader comes from legend—but in 2009, a team of Japanese archaeologists discovered what they thought could be the final resting place of the ancient queen. However, they can't know for sure without excavating the tomb—something the current emperor, himself a descendant of Himiko, has forbidden.

ABU BAKR

⟢ COMPASSIONATE CALIPH ⟢

Lifelong best friends Abu Bakr and Muhammad, the founder of Islam, did just about everything together. So when Muhammad revealed himself as the Prophet of God sometime in the seventh century A.D., Abu Bakr followed his friend faithfully into the religion of Islam. As the religion grew, so did Abu Bakr's reputation as Muhammad's chief adviser. The pair worked together to spread the Prophet's message until Muhammad grew ill. After Muhammad took his final breath on Earth, his best friend became the leader of the Islamic world.

As the first caliph, a spiritual and political leader, Abu Bakr continued Muhammad's life's work by spreading the word about Islam. He faced many challenges along the way, including fighting and winning a series of wars to bring a lasting Islamic influence across the Arabian Peninsula. But despite the turmoil of battle, he was regarded by his people as a just and compassionate ruler who treated all Muslims as equals.

Though he faced some strong opposition, Abu Bakr went on to extend both the political and spiritual influence of the Muslim community to all corners of the Middle East—and even took over some territory in the Byzantine Empire, the great power in the area during that time. Abu Bakr is also famous for commissioning a written record of sayings of the Prophet Muhammad, which became the Muslim sacred text still revered to this day: the Quran.

> **"Follow the way of life, which the Holy Prophet has shown you, for verily that is the right path."**
> —Abu Bakr

ROYAL RUNDOWN

➤ **BORN:** ca A.D. 573, Mecca, Arabia ➤ **DIED:** ca A.D. 634, Medina, Arabia ➤ **LED:** Rashidun Caliphate ➤ **REMEMBERED FOR:** The Quran and the spread of Islam through the Middle East

HENRY VIII

⊷╪═ SON-SEEKING SOVEREIGN ═══

In the 1520s, King Henry VIII of England found himself in a tight spot. His marriage to Catherine of Aragon, the daughter of the king and queen of Spain, held together an important alliance between England and Spain. But after 24 years together, the royal couple still did not have a male heir to inherit the throne. Though they did have a daughter, Mary, Henry was not going to be satisfied until he had a son to pass his crown to. Certain the pope would understand, Henry asked him to grant an annulment from Catherine. The pope said no—it was against the Catholic religion.

A fuming Henry decided to take matters into his own hands. As king, he proclaimed that England would no longer be a Catholic country. He went a step further by working with Parliament to establish the Church of England—and named himself as head of the new religion. Now Henry had the religious authority to grant himself the annulment. So, in 1533, that's what he did. He promptly married his next wife, Anne Boleyn. She, too, bore him a daughter: Elizabeth. Growing ever more desperate for a son, Henry falsely accused Anne of crimes including witchcraft and plotting to kill the king, and he had her arrested and beheaded.

Henry then moved on to his next wife, Jane Seymour, who finally gave him the son he had always wanted. Prince Edward was born in 1537, but the joy didn't last: Jane died just two weeks after giving birth. Henry went on to marry three more times before he died in 1547. As for his heirs, Edward was crowned king at age nine and ruled for six years before he fell ill. Then Henry's daughter Mary (who would famously become known as the cruel queen Bloody Mary) became the first queen of England and Ireland. Finally, the crown of England passed to Henry's other daughter, Elizabeth I—a ruler many consider one of the greatest monarchs in history.

Henry VIII was the first British king to be called "Your Majesty" instead of "Your Grace" or "Your Highness."

ROYAL RUNDOWN

➤ **BORN:** June 8, 1491, Greenwich, England ➤ **DIED:** January 28, 1547, London, England
➤ **LED:** England ➤ **REMEMBERED FOR:** Creating the Church of England

FIT FOR A KING

BOW DOWN TO THE CROWN!

Throughout history, kings around the globe have gotten creative with their crowns. Some were garnished with gold and gems galore; others were decked out in symbols and art; still others relied on animal accessories to make a unique fashion statement. No matter what their shape or size, these pieces of royal regalia really made a mark.

Crown of Christian IV, King of Denmark and Norway from 1588 to 1648

BRILLIANT BEADS

An intricate network of glass beads forming the shapes of animals, people, and other patterns adorns this colorful cone-shaped African crown, or *adenla*, of the Yoruba people of southwestern Nigeria, Benin, and Togo. Wearing the adenla signifies some serious sacred status: The birds mean that the king, or *oba*, is partly divine. And the beaded veil isn't just for decoration—it serves to protect the oba's subjects from their leader's supernatural powers, said to radiate from his face.

SYMBOLIC CIRCLET

Gifted to Stephen I (p. 12) by the pope more than 1,000 years ago and adorned with jewels and Byzantine art, the Holy Crown of Hungary is a priceless national symbol. So much so that during World War II, fearing it would be destroyed by the Nazis or Soviets, Hungary gave the crown to the United States for safekeeping. For 33 years it was kept secure at Fort Knox until 1978, when President Jimmy Carter (p. 133) returned the crown to Hungary.

FAN OF IRAN

Worn by reigning members of a former Iranian dynasty, the red velvet Kiani Crown is encrusted with 1,800 pearls, 300 emeralds, 1,800 rubies and spinels, and an unknown number of diamonds. The feathery-looking part of the topper, called an aigrette, can be removed from the headpiece by its butterfly-shaped base—in case the wearer needs to "dress down."

FINE AND FEATHERED

This eye-popping topper may have been worn by Moctezuma II, a 16th-century Aztec emperor who ruled over present-day Mexico. Likely the only one of its kind still intact, the massive headdress features more than a thousand solid gold plaques and plumes of many birds, from the cotinga to the kingfisher to the squirrel cuckoo. But what makes this piece truly head and shoulders above the rest is the display of almost 500 long, vibrant green tail feathers from the resplendent quetzal, a bird native to Central America and sacred to the ancient Aztec.

MILITARY
MASTERMINDS

Whether to head into battle or batten down the hatches on the home front is the hardest decision many kings ever had to make. Some trudged onto the battlefield as a last resort, carrying a heavy heart along with their weapons. Others made war a cornerstone of their reigns, putting their people in the line of fire in the name of expanding their empires. For good or evil, the art of battle has shaped the history of kingdoms—and defined the legacies of the kings who led them.

This art piece shows a scene from the Battle of Arsūf, where Richard I of England (p. 35) defeated the forces of Saladin (p. 34), leader of the Muslim army, in 1191.

GENGHIS KHAN

⟨= CONQUERING KING =⟩—○

Born into poverty amid the peaks and plateaus of Mongolia, Genghis Khan rose to build the largest empire there has ever been in the history of the world. He's one of the most controversial leaders of all time. Usually remembered as a killer, his reputation for violence was well earned. But there's much more to the story of Genghis Khan.

HUMBLE BEGINNINGS

Born around A.D. 1162 with the name Temujin, his family was a part of the Borjigin clan of the Mongols, the same people who would later lend their name to the country of Mongolia. They were a society of nomads who led herds of sheep across the grasslands, also called steppes, north of China and hunted with the help of trained golden eagles. But things were far from peaceful on the Mongolian steppes: The clans were constantly fighting, and Genghis Khan's childhood was marked by battles and bloodshed. When he was nine, his father was poisoned by an opposing clan, the Tatars. Genghis Khan was forced into exile along with his mother and six siblings. For a time, they lived a life of extreme poverty, sometimes scavenging roots to eat. When he was 20 years old, he was taken prisoner by a rival clan and enslaved before managing to escape his captors.

BUILDING A REPUTATION

In the years that followed, Genghis Khan slowly formed a group of followers and began taking vengeance on all the Mongols who had betrayed the Borjigin clan. He and his men attacked on horseback with lightning speed, letting loose arrows and javelins.

> "There is no good in anything until it is finished."
> —Genghis Khan

ROYAL RUNDOWN

➡ **BORN:** A.D. 1162, Mongolia ➡ **DIED:** August 18, 1227, Mongolia ➡ **LED:** Everything between the Aral and Yellow Seas ➡ **REMEMBERED FOR:** Amassing the largest land empire the world had ever seen

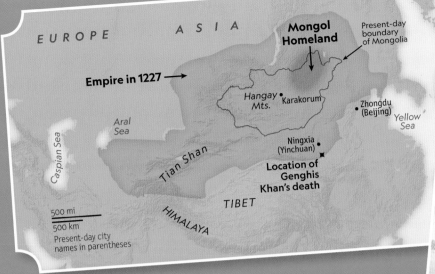

After every victory, they grew stronger. Each time he conquered a tribe, Genghis gave the people a choice: die, or join his army and fight for him. Most chose to fight, and by 1206, Genghis Khan had united all the nomadic tribes of Mongolia under his control.

But that wasn't enough for Genghis Khan. He wanted to take over the world. After carefully studying the new territories he hoped to conquer, he upgraded his troops from shooting arrows from the backs of Mongol horses to wielding weapons, like catapults, that could siege a city. He took over territory in huge swaths of China, along with what is now Turkmenistan, Uzbekistan, Afghanistan, and Iran. Before he died in 1227, he had amassed more than twice as much land as any other person in history—including famous conquerors like Julius Caesar (p. 53) and Alexander the Great.

Map of the Mongol Empire (Genghis Khan, circa 1206–1227) (above); a hunter on horseback holds a golden eagle in Mongolia

VICIOUS AND VICTORIOUS

There's no doubt Genghis Khan was a brutal ruler: It is estimated that his armies killed around 40 million people—about 10 percent of the world's total population at the time. But he also abolished torture and encouraged trade. He introduced all kinds of innovations to Eurasia, including pants, cannons, paper money, skis, and violins. He created one of the first worldwide postal systems, a network of mounted mail carriers carried messages across his empire by relay. Under his rule, arts and culture flourished. And, unlike many of history's empire builders, he was tolerant of the differing religions of his conquered people, enacting laws ensuring their freedom to worship as they wished. Though history's greatest conqueror was indeed a brutal warmonger, he also launched his kingdom into a new era and influenced the world for centuries to come.

COMMANDING QUEENS

THE AMAZONS
Warrior Women

Long before Genghis Khan waged war on the steppes of Eurasia, another kind of fighter ruled the area. Greek legends have long told of a group of fierce female warriors who lived together in a distant land. Now historians think they were real women, members of a nomadic people called the Scythians who ranged across Eurasia from about the ninth century B.C. to the first century B.C. When archaeologists excavated Scythian burial mounds beginning in the early 2000s, they found the remains of a horse-riding people who were clearly warriors buried alongside arrows, swords, daggers, spears, shields, and armor. At first, the scientists assumed these ancient soldiers must be male. But DNA testing revealed something shocking: About one-third of all the remains found belonged to women. Historians believe these ferocious, horse-riding fighters could be the real-life ancient warrior women behind the legend.

31

VIKING KINGS

Warriors From the Sea

Out of the icy mists of the north came the Vikings, Scandinavian people feared far and wide for their seafaring skills and their ferocity in battle. Vikings ruled seas and shores for more than 250 years, emerging from the ocean to attack cities and disappear back across the waves with their loot. Here are some of their most famous—and infamous—leaders.

WILD WARLORD:
Ívarr the Boneless (ca A.D. 794–873)

Many Viking kings had colorful names, but perhaps the most memorable belongs to Ívarr the Boneless. Truth mixes with legend in his history, but the stories say he was famous for his viciousness on the battlefield. The troop of Vikings he led—known as the Great Heathen Army—was notorious for its extraordinary cruelty. Ívarr himself was said to be a "berserker," a truly terrifying class of Viking warriors that would enter a trancelike state of uncontrollable rage when they fought. Tales say that on the way into battle, they would howl like wolves and attack anything within reach—boulders, trees, and sometimes each other. As for Ívarr's odd nickname, historians debate its origin. Some believe he had a bone disease that made him unable to walk; a few Norse accounts tell stories of Ívarr the Boneless being carried into battle on a shield while he shot at the enemy with arrows.

HAVOC WREAKER:
Eric Bloodaxe (ca A.D. 895–954)

Not all Vikings were ruthless brutes. But it's Vikings like Eric Bloodaxe that give the rest of them a bad reputation. Bloodaxe was willing to do anything to become the king of Norway—even kill his four older brothers to win the crown. After clearing the path to the throne, Bloodaxe was exiled by his younger brother, Haakon the Good. But that didn't put an end to Bloodaxe's desire to rule. He and his followers boarded a ship, sailed to England, and took over the kingdom of Northumbria, just south of Scotland. He ruled there from A.D. 947 to 948 and from 952 to 954, taking a break in between to wreak havoc raiding villages across Scotland and Ireland. Bloodaxe had a death befitting a vicious king: He was killed in an ambush set by a competing monarch.

Some have called him England's greatest Viking king. Cnut (ka-NOOT) was the son of Sweyn Forkbeard, the Viking king of Denmark. In 1013, when he was a boy, Cnut set sail with his father to invade England. Forkbeard died shortly after, leaving Cnut—probably then just a teenager—to rule the newly conquered kingdom. He rose to the challenge. A series of battlefield victories secured Cnut's position as leader of both England and Denmark. In 1028, Cnut also conquered Norway, uniting these kingdoms along the North Sea into the largest empire Denmark has ever seen, before or since. Cnut proved to be not only a successful warrior but also a statesman as well. He established trade, grew his economy, and was tolerant of the Christian religion of many of his conquered subjects—even traveling to Rome to meet the pope.

FAR-FLUNG FIGHTER:
Harald Hardrada (A.D. 1015–1066)

Harald Hardrada had a taste for adventure from a young age. Though he was born in Norway, he spent much of his youth adventuring in faraway lands. At just 15 years old, Harald followed his half brother, King Olaf II Haraldsson of Norway, to war. But the tide of battle turned against Olaf's troops. He was killed in battle, and Hardrada, gravely injured, barely managed to escape with his life. He fled to Russia, where he met his future wife, the daughter of the grand prince, and then went south to the Byzantine Empire, in what is now northern Turkey. There, Hardrada enlisted in the army of Emperor Michael IV and fought as far away as Sicily in the middle of the Mediterranean Sea. Now a seasoned fighter, Hardrada returned to Norway in 1045 and claimed the throne for himself. By 1047, he was the undisputed ruler of Norway.

COMMANDING QUEENS

FIERCE AND FEARLESS
Freydís Eiríksdóttir
(ca A.D. 1000s)

Though she wasn't real royalty, few people in history exhibited the Viking spirit quite like Freydís Eiríksdóttir. She was the daughter of Erik the Red, the Viking who settled Greenland, and sister of Leif Erikson, who is believed to be the first European to establish a settlement in North America. Bravery must have run in the family: Eiríksdóttir traveled across the vast Atlantic Ocean to establish a trading relationship with the indigenous people of "Vinland," the Viking name for modern-day eastern Canada. According to the legends, the relationship turned sour when some of the native people approached the Vikings with the intent to attack. Though she was pregnant at the time, Eiríksdóttir ran out of her tent screaming and beat a sword against her chest. When the war party saw the fierce Viking woman, they fled in fright. Though it's a legend, this tale could be based in truth: DNA analysis of the bones of Vikings buried with their weapons suggests that some of the warriors were indeed women.

SALADIN

⟨══ HERO TO HIS PEOPLE ══╾─○

As a boy, Saladin was a devoted student. He paid close attention when his teachers talked about the First Crusade of 1098, when Christian invaders had marched into his homeland in the Middle East, conquering and slaughtering in an effort to take control of holy sites there. It was a lesson that would go on to define his life.

When Saladin was a bit older, he joined the army of Nūr al-Dīn, a Muslim military ruler who had become a hero among his people for organizing troops to mount an attack against the second wave of Christian invaders (called the Second Crusade). The Christians had been pushed back, but they still held the holy city of Jerusalem. Ever the good student, Saladin learned the art of warfare quickly. Nūr al-Dīn put Saladin—only 22 at the time—in charge of a campaign. Before long, Saladin was ruling Egypt on behalf of Nūr al-Dīn.

When Nūr al-Dīn died, Saladin marched his armies to Syria and took control there. As the sultan of Egypt and Syria, he used his new territory as a base to turn back the crusaders, finally defeating them once and for all in 1187. Then Saladin sent his troops toward Jerusalem and took the city back. He was merciful to Jerusalem's Christian citizens, giving them 40 days to pay a tribute in exchange for their freedom. After 88 years of Christian dominance, the holy city was back under Muslim control.

In 1189, the Third Crusade began, and Christian forces, led by King Richard I of England, invaded once again. Through some smart statesmanship, Saladin managed to keep command of Jerusalem, along with most of Syria and Palestine. For both his morality and his military skill, Saladin is remembered as one of the greatest Muslim leaders in history.

> "It is not the custom of kings to kill kings."
> —Saladin

ROYAL RUNDOWN

➜ **BORN:** ca A.D. 1137, Tikrit, Iraq ➜ **DIED:** March 4, 1193, Damascus, Syria ➜ **LED:** Much of modern-day Egypt and the Middle East ➜ **REMEMBERED FOR:** Taking back the city of Jerusalem from Christian Crusaders

RICHARD I

⊷⊢═ LION-HEARTED LEADER ═⊶

Outside the Houses of Parliament in London, England, stands a statue of a king with his sword raised high: Richard I. He's celebrated as one of the greatest monarchs in English history. But ruling was never Richard's first concern. He once said that he would have sold his whole country if he could have found a buyer. During the 10 years of his reign, he spent only a few months in England. The rest of the time, he was fighting.

By the time he was just 16 years old, Richard was commanding his own army. His reputation for bravery and skill on the battlefield grew, earning him his famous nickname: Richard the Lionheart. But Richard's family was in constant conflict.

In 1173, Richard joined with his brothers to rebel against their father, King Henry II, and overthrow the throne. It's rumored that their mother, Eleanor, was behind the plot to secure the crown for her children. King Henry put down the rebellion and put Eleanor in prison for the next 16 years. When Henry died in 1189, Richard inherited the throne and was crowned king.

But Richard's heart wasn't in ruling England. Soon after his coronation, Richard left for the Third Crusade. He had a new mission: take the Holy Land from the Muslim leader Saladin, who had captured Jerusalem in 1187 and put it under Christian control. Although he couldn't gain control of Jerusalem—the Third Crusade's main objective—the mission was a success in nearly every other way. Richard won almost every battle, but was forced to return home when he learned that the king of France was ransacking his lands in his absence. Richard declared a truce with Saladin, and in 1192, the man who would become famous as England's crusader king set sail for home.

Centuries after his death, Richard went on to become celebrated as a hero in the Robin Hood legends.

ROYAL RUNDOWN

⇒► **BORN:** September 8, 1157, Oxford, England ⇒► **DIED:** April 6, 1199, Châlus, France
⇒► **LED:** England ⇒► **REMEMBERED FOR:** His reputation as a crusader king

TURF **WARS**

Preparing for Battle

A lucky few kings led their kingdoms through long periods of peace, but many monarchs lived and died by the sword. During calmer times, princes and kings studied strategy and mastered maneuvers so they could be better prepared in times of war. Here are some of history's heaviest hitters.

FATHER OF MODERN WARFARE:
Gustav II Adolf (1594–1632)

When Gustav II Adolf inherited the Swedish throne at just 16 years old, he found himself at the helm of a country in turmoil. His father, King Charles IX, had stolen the throne from Gustav's cousin King Sigismund III, who ruled Poland, too. Gustav feared that the Polish army could invade at any time to try to take the country back. Unfortunately, Charles IX had also started wars with Russia and Denmark, so the troops Gustav needed for protection were strewn all over northern Europe.

Gustav sprang into action. Until his death on the battlefield in 1632, he lead his troops in battle after battle. Though he had little fighting experience, he learned fast. Gustav's military successes set Sweden up to be the dominant power in the region for the next century. He's widely regarded as one of the greatest military leaders in history, and his battle tactics were studied by generals who came after him—including Napoleon I.

REFORMED RULER:
Ashoka (ca 304 B.C.–ca 232 B.C.)

He was called Ashoka the Terrible, and this emperor of India deserved his nickname. When his father died, Ashoka killed many of his own half brothers to claim the throne. As emperor, he set out to conquer India. For eight blood-drenched years, Ashoka the Terrible waged nonstop war. He grew the Mauryan Empire from the north of the country all the way to Burma in the east and Iran in the west, conquering nearly all of southern

VANQUISHER OF ROME:
Alaric I (ca A.D. 370–410)

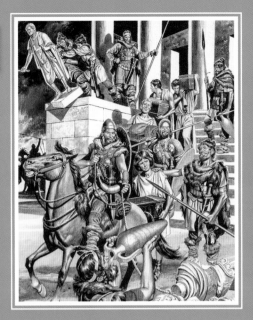

For centuries, the people of Rome lived protected behind the walls of their city. Though their army was constantly at war, fighting to expand the empire, Rome's brilliant military commanders had managed to stop invaders before they got too close to the capital. That changed when Alaric I came along.

Little is known about Alaric's early life. But we do know that before he became the leader of a group known as the Visigoths in A.D. 395, he had learned to fight as a soldier in the Roman army—the very one he would go on to defeat. Alaric led his people all around Europe, raiding cities and making off with their valuables. He successfully sacked the port of Athens, Corinth, and Sparta in Greece before setting his sights on Italy. In 410, he liberated tens of thousands of Roman slaves, then set siege to the city. For three days, Alaric's army plundered and left with enough wealth to buy their own country. It was the first time Rome had fallen in 800 years.

CONQUEROR OF EGYPT:
Piye (ca 775 B.C.–ca 719 B.C.)

Everybody knows about ancient Egypt, the civilization that flourished at the mouth of the Nile River for almost 3,000 years. But few have heard of another great ancient society just up the river. There, in modern-day Sudan, sat the kingdom of Kush.

In 730 B.C., the once all-powerful Egypt was crumbling. The civilization that had built the pyramids was being torn apart by warlords. In the chaos, one would-be tyrant named Tefnakht rose to power and began conquering territory left and right. But then he made a mistake: He decided to invade the kingdom of Kush, from his base of power in the Nile Delta. Kush's ruler, Piye, wasn't about to submit. He put together an army and marched north to meet Tefnakht. He crushed Tefnakht's commanders and then set about taking over the cities Tefnakht had captured, one by one. After just a few years, Piye had defeated Tefnakht and conquered one of the oldest and most celebrated civilizations in the world.

Immediately after his victory, he loaded up his ships with the finest jewels and horses and sailed back up the river to his homeland, never to return again.

India along the way. When he was finished, his empire was India's dominant power between 322 B.C. and 185 B.C.

But when Ashoka walked through the ancient territory of Kalinga the day after conquering it, something in him changed. An estimated 150,000 had died in his assault, and Ashoka was horrified with the amount of bloodshed. In that moment, he went from warmonger to peaceful leader. He devoted himself to Buddhism and nonviolence. He built wells, hospitals, and other public works to make life better for the people he had conquered. Once brutal on the battlefield, Ashoka became so devoted to the pursuit of peace that he put all kinds of animals under official protection—including squirrels and pigeons!

The Lion Capital of Ashoka—a sculpture of four lions standing back to back—was placed on top of one of the pillars erected by Ashoka throughout India during his reign.

THE ART OF **WAR**

Ask the world's top leaders what they consider the best management book of all time and the answer might surprise you: Many might name a slim volume called *The Art of War.* But it's far from a brand-new best seller; it was written more than 2,500 years ago! Since then, this masterpiece of military science has been used by more than just warlords: Leaders from generals to business executives to basketball coaches have studied the famous text to learn how to command a team—and win.

Divided into 13 chapters on 13 aspects of warfare, *The Art of War* is the oldest surviving military treatise in the world. Scholars long believed it was written by a Chinese military leader named Sun Tzu in the fourth or fifth century B.C. Today, many people think that Sun Tzu may not have been a real person: Instead, *The Art of War* might be a collection of greatest-hits strategies from many of China's best generals.

For more than 1,000 years after *The Art of War* was written, emperors and scholars across Asia consulted it when plotting takeovers, conquests, and military maneuvers. It was an especially big hit among Japanese samurai. Back then, the text was typically written on pieces of sewn-together bamboo. It reached the Western world at the end of the 18th century, when a missionary discovered the manuscript and translated it into French. The book remains a best seller to this day. It can be found in the briefcases and backpacks of business students, lawyers, CEOs, and coaches all over the world. So what does this cult classic of conflict have to say? Here are a few teachings from the ancient handbook of battle tactics:

Painting of Sun Tzu (above); a wooden types version of *The Art of War* (below)

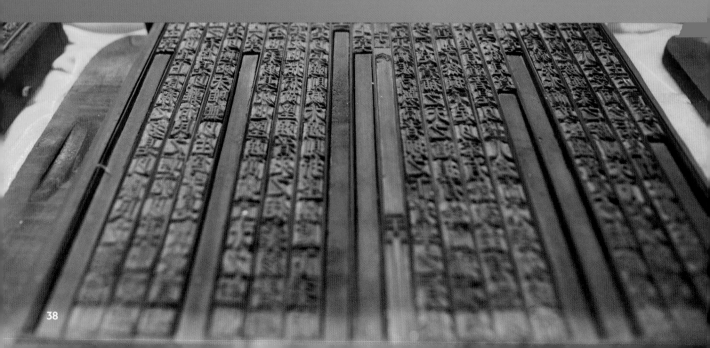

1. THE BEST BATTLE STRATEGY is to avoid fighting in the first place

"The supreme art of war is to subdue the enemy without fighting," reads *The Art of War.* Battle causes great hardship, and the greatest military strategists know that war is a last resort. If there's a way to achieve your goal through compromise or new strategies, take it.

Bamboo slips of *The Art of War* on display at the Military Museum of the Chinese People's Revolution in Beijing, China, in 2008

2. THE BATTLE IS WON before it begins

Planning is everything. Sun Tzu knew that it didn't matter how skilled his fighters were: If he had not thought through every possible move his enemies might make before the fighting began, he could still be defeated by a surprise attack.

LESSONS FROM *THE ART OF WAR*

3. BREAK IT DOWN

Commanding an army of 100,000 men seems like an impossible task, says Sun Tzu. The solution? Simple, he says. Break down your massive army into small, manageable groups. In the same way, any seemingly insurmountable task can be conquered if it is divided into small steps.

4. BE FLEXIBLE

No matter how much you prepare, it's inevitable that circumstances will change when you're in the heat of battle. Sun Tzu describes how, time and time again, he was faced with unexpected bad weather and poor battlegrounds. But don't give up, he says: Find a way to adapt.

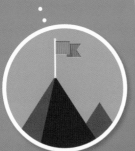

5. BELIEVE IN YOURSELF

It's impossible to succeed if you don't think you can do it. Once you've prepared for every possible obstacle and practiced your maneuvers until they are second nature, victory is possible only if you believe that you're capable of carrying out the challenge.

Sun Tzu statue in Shandong, China

SHAKA

⇥ KING OF THE ZULU ⇥

> "Up! Children of Zulu, your day has come. Up! And destroy them all."
> —Shaka

Born to a tiny tribe in southern Africa, shunned by his family, and treated as an outcast, Zulu chief Shaka would defy all the odds and grow up to become one of history's toughest warrior kings. Though his life ended in tragedy, in his time he rewrote the rules of war and forged a mighty empire.

A WARRIOR IS BORN

Shaka was born the son of Senzangakhona, the king of the Zulu, and Nandi, a princess from a neighboring clan. But his parents' marriage eventually fell apart. Shaka and his mother were cast out of Zululand and sought shelter with Nandi's people, the Langeni clan. Unfortunately for Shaka, he was bullied there because he was an exiled prince—someone who could have been powerful found himself totally powerless.

In 1802, the Langeni drove Nandi and Shaka out. They finally found a home with the Mthethwa tribe. An accomplished warrior named Dingiswayo ruled the new tribe and taught Shaka how to fight. Shaka discovered he had a talent for battle and devoted himself to improving his skills. He had a blacksmith forge him a spear, and when he found that he was more agile barefoot, he went without shoes to toughen up his feet for fighting. His devotion soon paid off: Shaka became a commander in Dingiswayo's army.

THE RETURN OF THE KING

When Senzangakhona died, in 1816, Shaka seized the opportunity to take over his father's kingdom. He left Dingiswayo's army and went to the Zulu territory on the White Umfolozi River. At that time, it's estimated that the Zulu numbered fewer than 1,500: They were one of the smallest and least powerful clans in the region. But from the moment Shaka took control, that began to change.

Shaka updated his soldiers' weapons, getting rid of their frail, long

ROYAL RUNDOWN

➤ **BORN:** ca 1787, South Africa   ➤ **DIED:** September 22, 1828, South Africa   ➤ **LED:** Zulu Empire
➤ **REMEMBERED FOR:** Increasing the size and power of the Zulu and his innovative military tactics

throwing spears and replacing them with assegais: swordlike weapons that gave them a huge advantage in close combat. He divided his army into regiments and devised battle tactics. Then, with a modernized army at his command, Shaka began conquering nearby clans, including the Langeni, the one that had bullied him as a boy.

Shaka and his Zulu warriors took over clan after clan and expanded his empire by offering tribes the opportunity to submit. Those who did became Zulu. Those who refused were either killed or chased off their land. Less than a year after Shaka took over with his new weapons and battle strategies, the Zulu Empire had quadrupled in size. By 1823, Shaka controlled all of the modern-day South African province of KwaZulu-Natal.

FALL OF A KING

In 1827, Shaka's beloved mother, Nandi, died. The loss completely unraveled the once successful and single-minded king. Consumed by grief, the king ordered the deaths of 7,000 of his own people. He outlawed the planting of crops, dooming the rest to starvation. Then Shaka tried to order his army to go raid in the north, but they had just gotten back from raiding in the south. It was a soldier's sacred right to have a season of rest, but Shaka ordered them gone anyway.

It was the last straw. On September 22, Shaka's two half brothers assassinated him to save the Zulu. It was a sad end for a king who had once risen from nothing to lead his people to greatness.

Zulu men performing a *ngoma*, a traditional dance, in South Africa (above); depiction of a Zulu village (left)

SHAKA'S BULL HORN FORMATION

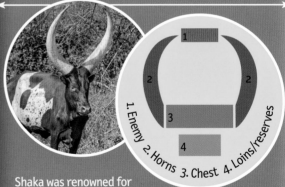

1. Enemy 2. Horns 3. Chest 4. Loins/reserves

Shaka was renowned for his military maneuvers, and the most famous of all was the bull horn formation. Shaka would direct his strongest fighters to make up a central "chest" of the bull. They would charge at the enemy and fight in close combat to pin down the opposing soldiers. Meanwhile, the two "horns" would race around to attack the enemy from behind. A reserve troop, known as the "loins," sat ready nearby to reinforce any part of the formation if it became weak. This simple yet brilliant strategy would go on to become a famous battlefield tactic.

41

REPRESSING **REVOLT**

Kings Who Quelled Rebellions

Some of history's most popular stories feature a band of plucky rebels who overthrow more powerful forces. However, for the ruthless rulers they challenge, uprisings are a threat to their authority that must be crushed. Here are a few merciless military leaders who stomped out rebellions to hold on to their power—at any cost.

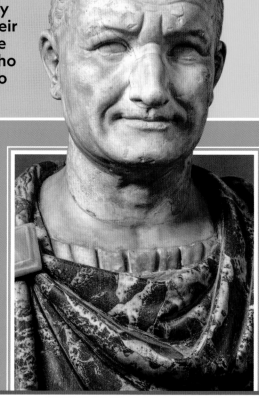

The Peasants vs. Richard II
(A.D. 1367–1400)

The Hundred Years' War between England and France stretched from the middle of the 14th century to the middle of the 15th century. During this long period of strife, kings on both sides found that the cost of fighting had drained their treasuries. One was Richard II of England. His kingdom nearly bankrupt, he resorted to increasing taxation on England's peasants. But the peasants—who had already suffered through two tax increases since the start of the war—had had enough. Led by a man named Wat Tyler, the peasants of southeastern England marched on London in 1381. The revolt started out triumphant. The rebels successfully sacked the fabled Tower of London—a feat never to be repeated in history. But Richard II struck back with a fury. Wat Tyler was killed in the counterattack, and without their leader, the peasants returned to the countryside.

The Zealots vs. Vespasian
(A.D. 9–79)

As Rome's borders expanded, more and more non-Romans were folded into the empire. The leaders of these kingdoms were removed, and the emperor appointed new Roman governors to rule in their place. In Roman-occupied Israel, Governor Gessius Florus angered the Israelites when he raised taxes and interfered in the religious practices of the Jewish citizens. In A.D. 66, Florus made things worse when he stole silver from the Temple, the holiest site in Judaism at the time. One group of Jews, known as the Zealots, revolted. They expelled the small force of Roman soldiers stationed in the city of Jerusalem, and for a moment, it looked as if they had a real chance to declare independence. But then the emperor sent an army commanded by the general Vespasian to put a stop to the rebellion. For three years, Vespasian besieged the city, gradually wearing down Jerusalem's defenses until the Zealots were defeated.

The Rebel Princes vs.
Emperor Jingdi of Han (188 B.C.–141 B.C.)

The Han dynasty, the royal family that ruled China from 206 B.C. through A.D. 9, brought about some of early China's greatest cultural achievements. Under the Han's dynasty's leadership, the Chinese invented paper and opened the Silk Road—the land-based trade route was incredibly important for the economies of Asia, the Middle East, and Europe for more than 1,300 years. But the dynasty was almost toppled in 154 B.C. when a group of princes rebelled against Emperor Jingdi. Jingdi's father, the previous emperor, had been forgiving of the princes who ruled the smaller states that made up his kingdom, allowing them to become nearly as powerful as the emperor himself. When Jingdi came to power, he tried to take back control—but seven of the princes weren't happy about it. They revolted against Jingdi, but they didn't succeed. With the help of his military genius general, Zhou Yafu, Jingdi defeated the princes and kept his hold on his empire.

The Gladiators vs.
Marcus Licinius Crassus (115 B.C.–53 B.C.)

Gladiators were famous for their willingness to fight to the death. But often they had no choice—these celebrated combatants of the Colosseum were slaves, the property of wealthy Romans. In the year 73 B.C., one such slave named Spartacus led a band of gladiators in a daring escape. They stole weapons and stormed the streets of a town called Capua. Over the next three years, the group of 200 runaway slaves grew to 120,000. Embarrassed by their inability to stop the gladiator rebels, the Roman Senate called in general Marcus Licinius Crassus. Crassus marched his legion south and trapped Spartacus and his rebels against the sea. Though the brave gladiators fought hard, Crassus and his soldiers defeated the rebels and ended the uprising. Crassus went on to briefly rule Rome as a member of the First Triumvirate, along with Pompey the Great and Julius Caesar (p. 53).

The Revolutionaries vs.
Catherine the Great
(1729–1796)

COMMANDING QUEENS

When nearby countries began taking over Polish territory in 1772, Tadeusz Kościuszko looked around for help. He traveled to France, where the earliest rumblings of revolution were quietly spreading, then the United States, where rumblings had given way to an all-out war. Then he returned to his homeland of Poland, where Catherine the Great, empress of Russia, was invading to prevent a revolution there. Kościuszko fought back, leading Polish peasants armed with farming sickles to a stunning victory against the Russian army, and then went on to defend the capital, Warsaw, from siege. Catherine quashed the rebellion, just one of a dozen such uprisings she put down during her reign. Brilliant and ambitious, Catherine stopped at nothing to build Russia into a world power. She grew her territory and turned her dominion into one of Europe's most powerful empires, but her conquests often came at the expense of her people, who suffered under the hardships of war.

HŌJŌ TOKIMUNE

⚔ JAPAN'S PROTECTOR ⚔

In the 13th century, most of Asia, the Middle East, and Europe were being trampled under the hooves of the vast army of mounted Mongolian fighters led by Kublai Khan, the grandson of Genghis Khan (p. 30). But the geography of Japan, a nation spread out over a chain of islands, had kept it safe from attackers ... so far.

The ruler of those lucky islands, Hōjō Tokimune, was only 17 when he came to power. But he wasn't one to be intimidated. Kublai Khan, who led China, Mongolia, and much of the known world at that time, sent Tokimune a message demanding that Japan submit to him and pay him yearly taxes. Fearing the power of the khan, many in the Japanese court urged Tokimune to submit. But Tokimune refused. If the khan wanted Japan, his horses had better learn to swim.

Kublai Khan went on the attack. In 1274, he sent a force 25,000 strong across the sea. His soldiers succeeded in capturing a few barrier islands, but before they could mount a decisive invasion, a storm forced the fleet to return to mainland Asia.

One close call was enough for Tokimune. Determined to deter future attacks, he ordered the construction of state-of-the-art defenses along western Japan, complete with seawalls to make landing ships more difficult. In 1281, Kublai Khan put the system to the test. He sent a huge army—nearly 140,000 soldiers—straight at the heart of Japan. But the defenses held, once again aided by the weather—this time, a timely typhoon that destroyed the invading fleet. Having witnessed two acts of Mother Nature saving his people from war, Tokimune decided to devote his life to spreading the principles of Zen Buddhism, a philosophy that aims to help people find meaning and peace.

The Hōjō family ruled Japan for more than 130 years.

ROYAL RUNDOWN

➜ **BORN:** June 5, 1251, Kamakura, Japan ➜ **DIED:** April 20, 1284, Kamakura, Japan
➜ **LED:** Japan ➜ **REMEMBERED FOR:** His dramatic defiance of a warmonger

HAILE SELASSIE I

⊷⊨ ETHIOPIA'S LAST EMPEROR ⊨

Born Tafari Makonnen in 1892, Haile Selassie was a son of Ras Makonnen, a chief adviser and cousin to Ethiopia's emperor, Menelik II. Tafari, whose intelligence as a young man impressed even the emperor, seemed determined to rise to prosperity and bring his country along with him. When he himself became emperor of Ethiopia, he made it his life's mission to help his country gain a foothold in the modern world.

Selassie came to power in 1917, through a series of power grabs that left him as regent and heir, ruling in the place of the previous king's young daughter. By 1923, he had led Ethiopia to join the League of Nations, an international organization that worked to resolve disputes between countries. The next year, when he visited Europe, he became the first Ethiopian leader to travel abroad. His efforts made him beloved by Ethiopia's young people as a symbol of progress. And when the young empress-to-be died in 1930, Selassie became emperor.

But as World War II approached, Selassie found himself and his blossoming country abandoned by the global community. On top of that, Italy—which had once tried and failed to invade Ethiopia—had a new leader: dictator Benito Mussolini. When Mussolini began forming plans to invade Ethiopia once more, Selassie begged for help from France and Britain, but they wouldn't stand up to the Italian tyrant.

Mussolini's forces crossed into Ethiopia in 1935. They toppled the capital, Addis Ababa, and Selassie was forced to flee. But even while in exile in Great Britain, he never gave up his cause. He pleaded for help from the British government, and in 1941, he finally got it. Selassie returned to his homeland with the Allied forces behind him. Within months, the Italians were finally defeated, and Selassie returned to rule Ethiopia for another 33 years.

> "Peace demands the united efforts of us all. Who can foresee what spark might ignite the fuse?"
> —Haile Selassie I

ROYAL RUNDOWN

⇒ **BORN:** July 23, 1892, Ejersa Goro, Ethiopia ⇒ **DIED:** August 27, 1975, Addis Ababa, Ethiopia ⇒ **LED:** Ethiopia ⇒ **REMEMBERED FOR:** Securing support in a counterattack against Italian invaders

FIT FOR A KING

FORMIDABLE FORTRESSES

Castles served as homes, fortresses, and symbols of power for mighty monarchs and their lords throughout history. As early as 1,000 years ago, these structures began to pop up all over the world—not just in Europe but also in Africa, Japan, India, and Korea. One castle could protect a 10-mile (16-km) radius, so kings often constructed many to watch over their realms. Every last detail about castles was built with defense in mind, from their strategic location, to the materials used to make them, and even the inclusion of sneaky spaces used for quick getaways.

MOAT

The moat was a castle's first line of defense. Not all castles had them, but some that did filled these deep trenches with up to 30 feet (9 m) of water to keep enemies out. Unlike what you may have seen in movies, there were no angry alligators swimming through these waters: Moats were used as the castle garbage dump and were a place for emptying toilets. Yuck! Moats that stayed dry were fashioned to be intimidating in other ways: Some were filled with sharp spikes or—in the case of one especially terrifying moat in the Czech Republic—filled with bears!

GATEHOUSE

Gatehouse guards were in charge of raising the drawbridge and lowering the portcullis, a heavy gate that protected the front entrance. Gatehouses also had a built-in secret weapon: gaps in the ceiling above the gatehouse, allowing defenders to unleash arrows at trespassers and even dump boiling water, hot sand, or other scalding substances on the advancing enemy.

CRENELLATIONS

Ever wonder why castles have those rectangular gap-toothed patterns on the tops of their walls and towers? They're called crenellations, and the design isn't just for decoration. Crenellations gave archers a defensive barrier to hide behind and a narrow opening from which they could fire arrows.

WALLS

Most castle walls actually consisted of at least two sturdy stone barriers. The outer, or "curtain," walls could be up to 30 feet (9 m) high and as thick as three king-size mattresses! Some went even further: Krak des Chevaliers, a castle in Syria, had walls up to 80 feet (24 m) thick. Many walls also had "arrow loops" cut into them. Defenders could fire arrows through these vertical slits without getting hit themselves.

STAIRCASES

The dedication to defense made its way inside the castle itself. When all else failed, the king and his crew could flee farther into his fortress by way of spiral staircases. These stairwells were often built clockwise from the ascender's point of view. This was important, because defenders standing on the upper stairs looking down could easily use their right arm—which typically held their sword—to slash at enemies clambering up. They just had to hope their attacker wasn't left-handed and able to swing past this clever architectural strategy!

STORMING **THE CASTLE**

Throughout history, people devised ingenious—and deadly—technologies to get past even the sturdiest of castle walls. These devices could fling projectiles, like rocks and boulders, over long distances. That type of force could make a king's walls come crashing down.

Catapult

One of the most famous siege weapons was the catapult. The catapult was a slingshot-like weapon that consisted of a bucket attached to a long arm that was winched down with materials like leather or sometimes even horse hair. The materials would twist, creating tons of tension. When that tension was released—*whoosh!* But rocks weren't the only things clever besiegers tossed at their enemies. In 184 B.C., military leader Hannibal of Carthage catapulted jars filled with venomous snakes onto his enemies' ships. His opponents ultimately retreated.

Trebuchet

Another piece of wily weaponry used during sieges was the trebuchet, a massive, injury-inducing war machine that worked like a seesaw, using counterweights to hurl everything from 300-pound (136-kg) stones, flaming barrels of tar, sharp wooden poles, and even manure at castle walls. Trebuchets were so precise and powerful that some even had nicknames, including "Earthquake's Daughters," "Big Mother," and "Bad Neighbor."

CHAPTER THREE

RULERS IN REVOLUTION

Some kings come to power at a tipping point. Their countries teeter on the brink of change, with the nobles restless, the people angry, and invaders at their doorsteps. Great leaders rise to the occasion, guiding their kingdoms through upheaval and ushering in eras. Other monarchs fail to weather the storm of revolution: Their subjects rebel and the rulers are forced to give up the crown and flee. No matter what the outcome, revolution is a true test of a monarch's leadership. These are some of history's most remarkable rulers during times of turbulence.

Painting depicting members of a Philippine revolutionary society opposing Spanish colonialism in the Philippines

WILLIAM III

━━ THE GLORIOUS REVOLUTIONARY ━━

> "No office ennobles its possessors."
> —William III

The second half of the 17th century was a time of great upheaval in Europe. People warred over religious differences and fought over territory. It was during this turning point in history that William III came to power. By the end of his reign, William had preserved the crown of England while fostering the beginnings of a new era of rule by government that still exists today.

RISE TO POWER

William III was born at a time of crisis in his homeland of the Netherlands. His mother's bedroom was draped in black to mourn his father, William II, who had died just eight days earlier. In an attempt to seize power, William II's enemies passed an act that decreed no one in William's family, the House of Orange, could ever be in power again. But William was taught that he had been chosen by God to rule—something that likely weighed heavy on the young prince.

In the spring of 1672, the kings of England and France teamed up to invade the Netherlands. The Dutch navy put up a fight, but their troops on land were losing—and fast. As a last resort, the Dutch military flooded low-lying areas to make them tougher to invade, and William was assigned to defend them. Against all odds, he did. The public was so grateful to William for saving their home that they rose up to support him. On July 8, 1672, William III was proclaimed stadtholder, or head of state, of the Netherlands.

ROYAL RUNDOWN

➤ **BORN:** November 4, 1650, The Hague, Netherlands   ➤ **DIED:** March 8, 1702, London, England
➤ **LED:** The Netherlands, England, Scotland, and Ireland   ➤ **REMEMBERED FOR:** Establishing England's parliamentary government

BECOMING KING

In 1677, William married Mary II, the English daughter of James II, who later became the king of England. William was hoping the marriage would strengthen his influence in his wife's home country. There, revolution was brewing: King James II was a Catholic, but many of his people—along with his daughter Mary—were Protestant. The English people so hated their king that by 1687, many were begging William and Mary to step in.

On November 5, 1688, William and his army landed on English soil and marched to London. A government of James's opponents proclaimed William and Mary as joint monarchs of England, Ireland, and Scotland. The deposed King James fled to France. The takeover became known as the Glorious Revolution, and it ushered in a new era of rule. William and Mary accepted terms set by the English Parliament that decreed they would have less power than the monarchs that came before them. This was the beginning of England's parliamentary system of government, which is still in place today.

The new monarchs' power was tested the very next year, when James II landed in Ireland with an army of French soldiers behind him, ready to fight for his throne back. In response, William put together the largest troop of soldiers that had ever marched in Ireland. In 1690, he defeated James at the Battle of the Boyne. The victory is still celebrated in Northern Ireland today.

William III landed in Torbay, England, on November 5, 1688, leading 14,000 troops in an invasion of England.

END OF THE MONARCHY

After his success against the former king of England, William turned to defeating his other old enemy—the king of France. Louis XIV had been conquering territory around Europe, and William was determined to stop him. He skillfully negotiated an alliance between important kingdoms across Europe, then spent most of the next eight years on the battlefield, leaving his wife, Mary, to rule in his absence. In 1697, William succeeded, forcing Louis to surrender much of the land he had taken over.

But William's life ended in tragedy, just as it had begun. In 1694, Mary died from smallpox, and William never recovered from the shock. In 1702, William was badly injured when his horse tripped on a molehill, and he died from his fall a month later. While William III had enjoyed the support of most of England, there were those who had always hated that England had been handed over to a foreign leader. These men toasted the mole that dug the hill that killed the king, celebrating the death of a monarch who had changed their country forever.

POWERFUL CO-RULER
Mary II (1662–1694)

COMMANDING QUEENS

The marriage of William of Orange to Mary II, the daughter of King James II of England, didn't get off to a great start: It's said the bride spent the entire ceremony weeping! Mary might not have been happy about the union, but her nation saw the Protestant William as its ideal new king. Once the conspirators in England invited William to come take the English crown, Mary's religious beliefs compelled her to take the side of her Protestant husband, not her Catholic father. Mary insisted that they be crowned co-rulers, and while William was off fighting France, she controlled the country alone. Together, the two were held in such high esteem that, in 1693, the first college built in the English colony of Virginia was named for them: the College of William and Mary.

ET TU, BUDDY?

Kings Betrayed by Their Own People

Some kings were lucky enough to pass away peacefully in old age. Others died on the battlefield. But more than a few kings have been done in by the people they least suspected: their own subjects or trusted advisers. Here are a few rulers who met their fate at the hands of their own people.

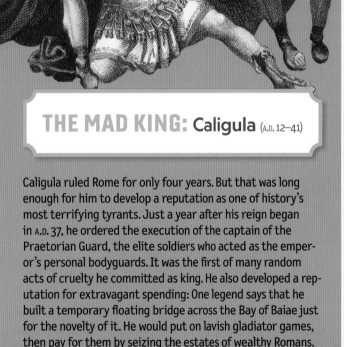

THE MAD KING: Caligula (A.D. 12–41)

Caligula ruled Rome for only four years. But that was long enough for him to develop a reputation as one of history's most terrifying tyrants. Just a year after his reign began in A.D. 37, he ordered the execution of the captain of the Praetorian Guard, the elite soldiers who acted as the emperor's personal bodyguards. It was the first of many random acts of cruelty he committed as king. He also developed a reputation for extravagant spending: One legend says that he built a temporary floating bridge across the Bay of Baiae just for the novelty of it. He would put on lavish gladiator games, then pay for them by seizing the estates of wealthy Romans. The people truly began to worry that their emperor had lost his mind after he marched his army all the way to the north coast of France with the intent to invade Britain—but then ordered his troops to stop and collect seashells on the beach instead. The Romans had had enough of their cruel and unpredictable tyrant: Caligula was murdered by his own Praetorian Guard while attending gladiator games.

THE END OF THE LINE: Xerxes I (ca 520 B.C.–465 B.C.)

Four years before Xerxes became king of Persia, in 486 B.C., his father, Darius I, had suffered a humiliating defeat at the hands of the Greek army at the Battle of Marathon. So Xerxes set out to avenge his father and achieve greatness for himself. In 484 B.C., he gathered an army of about 360,000 and led his troops into Greece. The most famous encounter of that war was the Battle of Thermopylae, when for three days a mere 300 Greek soldiers from Sparta brought the vast Persian advance to a complete halt. Though Xerxes was eventually able to annihilate the Spartan defenders and burn down the Greek capital of Athens, the war bankrupted Persia. It was the beginning of the end of the Achaemenid Empire. Back home, after two more decades of reckless spending, Xerxes' royal court could take no more. His own adviser, Artabanus, put Xerxes to death.

FORSAKEN BY A FRIEND:
Julius Caesar (100 B.C.–44 B.C.)

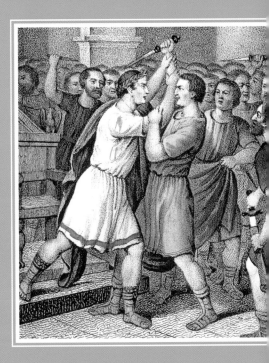

Julius Caesar was one of the greatest generals of the ancient world. He conquered territory after territory, turning Rome from a city into a mighty empire. Then, in 49 B.C., he saw an opportunity to rise to power: He led his troops right into Italy and invaded his own country. Luckily for Caesar, his plan worked. His fiercely loyal soldiers were able to defeat the forces of the Roman Senate. The defeated Senate reluctantly declared Caesar *dictator perpetuo*, dictator for life. As dictator, Caesar spent a lot of effort trying to win over the common people: He opened private libraries to the public, extended citizenship to newly conquered peoples in Gaul (an ancient region of western Europe), and even built shopping centers. But as much as the people loved Caesar, the Senate hated and feared him for turning their democracy into a dictatorship. So on March 15, 44 B.C., a group of senators famously ambushed and assassinated Caesar, putting an end to his reign. In playwright William Shakespeare's version of the events, when Caesar recognized his friend Brutus among the assassins, he said with shock and dismay, "Et tu, Brute?" meaning "And you, Brutus?"

FATHER OF AN EMPIRE:
Philip II (ca 382 B.C.–336 B.C.)

Philip II of Macedon is most often remembered as the father of Alexander the Great, one of history's most victorious conquerors. But Philip was a skilled military commander in his own right. When he was crowned king of Macedon in 359 B.C., his neighboring Greek city-states were constantly at war with each other. Around 367 B.C., Philip himself was captured and held hostage by the city-state of Thebes. But Philip was savvy, and he took advantage of his position inside enemy lines to observe Thebes's advanced battle tactics. When he was finally ransomed back to Macedonia, Philip immediately set about upgrading his military with state-of-the-art weapons like the *sarissa*, a 16-foot (5-m)-long thrusting spear. With his newly improved army behind him, Philip turned the tables on his former captors. By 337 B.C., he had either conquered or pressured nearly all of the Greek city-states into an alliance with him as the leader. Then, without warning, when the king was at the height of his power, he was mysteriously assassinated by one of his bodyguards, Pausanias. Prince Alexander inherited a powerful military and a united Greece, setting the stage for him to begin building his own empire.

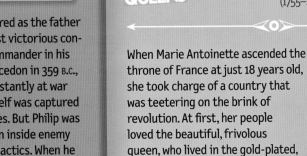

COMMANDING QUEENS

LAST QUEEN OF FRANCE
Marie Antoinette
(1755–1793)

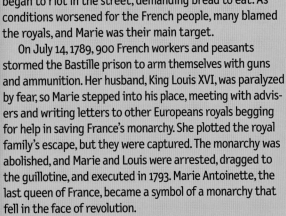

When Marie Antoinette ascended the throne of France at just 18 years old, she took charge of a country that was teetering on the brink of revolution. At first, her people loved the beautiful, frivolous queen, who lived in the gold-plated, velvet-draped Palace of Versailles. She spared no cost in indulging her expensive tastes—holding extravagant parties and often spending twice her annual clothing budget of about $3.6 million in today's money. But the French people—suffering under a bad harvest that had made the price of grain skyrocket—grew resentful of the royal family's spending. Hungry mobs began to riot in the street, demanding bread to eat. As conditions worsened for the French people, many blamed the royals, and Marie was their main target.

On July 14, 1789, 900 French workers and peasants stormed the Bastille prison to arm themselves with guns and ammunition. Her husband, King Louis XVI, was paralyzed by fear, so Marie stepped into his place, meeting with advisers and writing letters to other Europeans royals begging for help in saving France's monarchy. She plotted the royal family's escape, but they were captured. The monarchy was abolished, and Marie and Louis were arrested, dragged to the guillotine, and executed in 1793. Marie Antoinette, the last queen of France, became a symbol of a monarchy that fell in the face of revolution.

MARCUS AURELIUS

◄── RULING WITH REASON ═╾╌○

"To live happily is an inward power of the soul."
—Marcus Aurelius

By the time Marcus Aurelius came to power, Rome had dealt with its share of bad emperors. Many rulers were men who abused their power and spent the empire's treasury on themselves. But Marcus Aurelius was different. Hailed as one of the greatest emperors of the Roman Empire, he was a man of learning with a strong sense of duty.

Though he was the son of a distinguished Roman family, Aurelius was not in line to be emperor. He was fascinated with a type of philosophy called Stoicism, which emphasizes the importance of reason and restraint and rejects the trappings of wealth. His work ethic caught the attention of Emperor Hadrian. Hadrian was so impressed that he asked his adopted son, Antoninus Pius, to himself adopt Aurelius and name him his heir. At the age of 17, Aurelius began working alongside his adopted father, learning the ins and outs of government.

Antonius Pius became emperor upon the death of Hadrian in 138. After he died in 161, the crown passed to Marcus Aurelius. In an unusual move, Aurelius insisted that his adopted brother, Lucius Aurelius Verus Augustus, rule with him as co-regent. The two new emperors were tested through the 160s, when Rome battled with the nearby Parthian Empire for land, then had to fight off invading Germanic tribes. At first, Aurelius stayed home to rule while Verus went off to fight. But after Verus died in the conflict, Aurelius had to take to the battlefield himself. He led a Roman army out past the empire's frontier to strike back at the Germanic invaders. Between battles, he passed laws that improved the lives of slaves, widows, and young people.

While his campaign was a major success for the empire, Aurelius himself died of an illness in his war camp in 180. Though his reign was marked by incessant warfare, Aurelius is remembered for practicing the philosophy he preached: always putting the needs of his people ahead of his own desires for glory. Students of philosophy still study his collection of thoughts on self-discipline, morality, and strength, called the *Meditations*.

ROYAL RUNDOWN

⇒ **BORN:** April 26, A.D. 121, Rome, Italy   ⇒ **DIED:** March 17, A.D. 180, Vindobona, Austria
⇒ **LED:** Roman Empire   ⇒ **REMEMBERED FOR:** Philosophical *Meditations*

AKBAR THE GREAT

⊙≡ STRIVING FOR PEACE ≡►

Akbar the Great became king of a handful of small lands in northern India when he was just 14 years old. He set about waging war and created the mighty Mogul Empire. But Akbar didn't become famous for his military prowess alone; he was also known for his enlightened treatment of those he conquered.

As good as he was at winning battles, Akbar was far better at knowing which battles were *worth* fighting. His opening move as king secured the Moguls' control of trade routes in the region and provided them with access to rich farmlands. With the region's economy and agriculture under Mogul control, Akbar was able to send a well-fed and well-armed military into a confrontation with the infamous Rajputs, fierce Hindu warriors who had given Akbar's Muslim ancestors no end of trouble.

After proving themselves evenly matched, Akbar and the Rajput king agreed to stop fighting. Akbar married a Rajput princess, and the two peoples were united. Once the fighting was done, Akbar managed to do something no other Muslim ruler in India had been able to do: He led peacefully. He did this by showing his Hindu neighbors respect and tolerance. Akbar appointed Rajputs to some of the highest levels of his government. He also allowed the Hindus to practice their religion and would even join them in celebrating some of their festivals.

During the rest of his reign, it became Akbar's mission to make his empire the envy of the rest of the world. He devoted himself to filling his kingdom with buildings of astounding size and beauty. One of his crowning achievements is the Red Fort in the city of Agra. Its more than 500 pavilions are decorated with intricate carvings, screens, and paintings. Agra became the home base for one of the greatest empires of the medieval world.

> The Mogul Empire tripled in wealth and size during Akbar's reign.

ROYAL RUNDOWN

➤ **BORN:** October 15, 1542, Umerkot, Pakistan ➤ **DIED:** October 27, 1605, Fatehpur Sikri, India
➤ **LED:** Mogul Empire ➤ **REMEMBERED FOR:** Making peace with the Rajputs and establishing the city of Agra

COMEBACK KINGS

Down but Not Out

It's not easy being king—and it's even harder *staying* king. Whether by war, revolution, or a change in popular opinion, many of history's rulers found themselves overthrown or cast out. But sometimes, they came back again. Here are a few kings who lost their throne, only to reclaim it— some of them more than once!

RETURN OF THE KING: Ferdinand I (1751–1825)

Ferdinand I wore two separate crowns: one for Naples and one for Sicily. Today, both are regions in modern Italy, but then they were separate kingdoms. Ferdinand ruled during the 1700s, a time when monarchs were becoming unpopular with the people. This was the era of the French Revolution, when the French people—tired of paying taxes to fund the crown's extravagant lifestyle while the people went hungry— rebelled against their king, Louis XVI (p. 62), and spread the seeds of revolt around the world.

Ferdinand condemned the uprising of the French people and their ideas and spent 23 years fighting France's new revolutionary armies. In 1796, Napoleon Bonaparte marched into central Italy, kicked Ferdinand out, and, by 1799, had established his own government: the Parthenopean Republic. That same year, Ferdinand managed to march back in and take over, only to be driven out again six years later by another of Napoleon's armies, this one led by his brother Joseph. Joseph Bonaparte claimed the crowns of Naples and Sicily until 1815, when France was defeated by Austria at the Battle of Tolentino, the decisive skirmish in the Neapolitan War. Finally, Ferdinand was back on the throne—and this time he wasn't taking any chances. Ferdinand abolished the constitutional government and declared himself an absolute monarch, Ferdinand I of the Two Sicilies.

PRESIDENT PART II:
Grover Cleveland (1837–1908)

In democracies like the United States, leaders rise and fall by the ballot box. Nobody knew that lesson better than Grover Cleveland, America's only president to be voted out of office, then, four years later, voted back in.

President Cleveland believed that a president's job was to protect the U.S. Treasury from reckless spending. Because of this, he spent his first term doing little more than exercising his presidential power to

EMPEROR AGAIN:
John V Palaeologus (1332–1391)

John V Palaeologus of the Byzantine Empire, the eastern part of the Roman Empire in what is now Turkey, spent his entire life fighting to stay on his throne. He was only eight years old when his father died, and it took two civil wars before John V was recognized as the Byzantine emperor. After the first, John V briefly had a co-emperor, his father's former adviser, Cantacuzenus. After the second, John V ousted Cantacuzenus and ruled all on his own.

But his struggle for the throne wasn't over. Soon, John V found himself facing the looming power of the Ottoman Turks, a new group that threatened his empire. If that wasn't bad enough, John V's children and grandchildren were getting power-hungry. His own son, Andronicus IV, ousted John V from the throne in 1376. John V managed to take it back—only to be deposed again in 1390 by his grandson John VII. John V was restored once again later that year and died as emperor in 1391. Just 60 years after his death, the Byzantine Empire collapsed once and for all when the Ottomans finally took control, in 1453.

ROYAL REBOUND:
Stanislaw I (1677–1766)

When Stanislaw Leszczyński (lesh-TINK-skee) was a young man, his homeland of Poland was caught in the middle of a continent-wide game of military maneuvering. Sweden, France, Austria, and Russia were all plotting to put different people on the Polish throne. In 1709, King Charles XII of Sweden invaded Poland, forced the Polish nobility to remove the current monarch, King Augustus II, and installed Stanislaw, the son of a powerful Polish family, as king.

Before Stanislaw had time to do much of anything, Russian forces chased Sweden out of Poland, leaving Stanislaw without support. He fled to France. Backed by Russia, King Augustus II was able to reclaim the throne. But after Augustus II died of old age, Stanislaw saw his chance. He donned a disguise and traveled to Poland, where he became king again—only this time, he was elected by the people. His celebration didn't last long. Once again, Russia and Austria invaded and ousted him from the throne. After five more years of conflict, a new king ruled Poland, but Stanislaw was allowed to keep his royal titles and a lifetime ownership of several Polish provinces. Considering he was never meant to be king, that seems like a good deal!

veto—meaning when bills came to his desk to be signed, he would refuse. President Cleveland vetoed 414 bills, twice as many as all the previous presidents combined! But many thought he went too far when he vetoed a bill that would have provided payment to U.S. Civil War veterans. Cleveland lost the election of 1888 and had to leave the White House. The next president, Benjamin Harrison, had the opposite problem—he was deeply unpopular for what many saw as overspending government money. Americans were again ready for a president who would keep a tight watch on the nation's purse strings. There, waiting in the wings, was Grover Cleveland. He won an easy victory in the 1892 election and resumed his position as defender of the Treasury.

REVOLUTION IN THE PHILIPPINES

⟨ THE BATTLE FOR INDEPENDENCE ⟩

Many people know the story of the American Revolutionary War, when plucky colonists fought off the British redcoats and devoted their new country to life, liberty, and the pursuit of happiness. But it might come as a surprise to some to learn that at one point America sat on the other side of the table—as the country that refused to let go of one of its colonies. This is the story of Philippine independence.

1,000 YEARS AGO

The Philippines is a land with its own language and culture, and it takes part in vibrant trade with other Southeast Asian countries.

500 YEARS AGO

During the Age of Exploration, Europeans begin traveling the world by sea in search of new trading routes—and countries they can take over. Spain claims the Philippines, which still bears the name of the Spanish king Philip II to this day.

1892

By the late 19th century, the Filipino people have been wanting independence for decades. Their murmurs of revolution turn into action when a secret group called the Katipunan begins planning a rebellion.

1896

Spain discovers the plot and sends in troops. Battles break out on the island of Luzon, and 28-year-old Emilio Aguinaldo becomes leader of the Filipino fighting force. The Philippine Revolution begins.

Funerary mask from the Butuanon culture, a people who lived in the Philippines as early as the 9th century

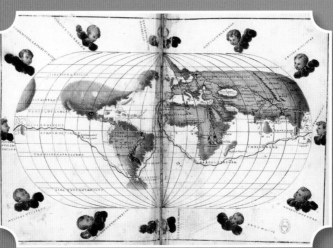

Map showing the route of Ferdinand Magellan, the first recorded European to reach the Philippines

In April, another war begins—this time, over Spain's brutal obliteration of a revolution in Spanish-controlled Cuba. America steps in to intervene on behalf of the revolutionaries, and on May 1, 1898, the Spanish-American War begins.

By August, Filipino freedom fighters have Spanish ground forces surrounded—but then the American military arrives. They destroy the Spanish fleet and take over the capital city of Manila. On December 10, Spain hands control of the Philippines over to the United States.

President-elect Manuel Roxas of the Philippines (right) is greeted by U.S. president Harry Truman during his visit to the White House on May 10, 1946.

Revolutionary leader Emilio Aguinaldo is captured in March 1901, and the war officially ends in July 1902.

Though the United States often promises the Filipinos more power to rule themselves, the islands remain under American control until World War II.

When the war is over, the United States finally agrees to grant the Philippines full independence on July 4, 1946—a date mirroring its own Independence Day.

1898

EARLY 1900s

1946

1899

The United States may have captured Manila, but Filipino forces control the rest of the island chain. They refuse to recognize United States rule, and the Philippine-American War begins.

WORLD WAR II

Japanese forces invade the Pacific, capturing the Philippines in the process. America fights back for control of the islands, and by 1944, American forces retake the Philippines.

1962

President Diosdado Macapagal changes the country's official Independence Day to June 12—to honor the day in 1898 that the country declared its freedom from Spain after 300 years of colonial rule.

SIMÓN BOLÍVAR

⚔ HERO OF A REVOLUTION ⚔

At the height of its power, around 1790, the Spanish Empire was a globe-spanning superpower. But circumstances aligned that ended nearly 300 years of Spanish dominance: At home, Spain was facing the onslaught of France in the Napoleonic Wars. Overseas, colonists were beginning to clamor for the same independence recently won by the United States. One man would help inspire several South American colonies to revolt against Spain. He was Simón Bolívar.

> "An ignorant people is the blind instrument of its own destruction."
> —Simón Bolívar

A TASTE FOR REVOLUTION

Simón Bolívar was born to one of the wealthiest families in the South American city of Caracas, the capital of Venezuela, but both his parents died before he was 10 years old. While he had some other family and a string of tutors, there was no one to keep him in line, and the young Bolívar ran wild. That is, until one tutor came along: Simón Rodríguez, who introduced Bolívar to radical new ideas on self-governance.

By 1804, Bolívar was well educated, wealthy, and ready for an adventure. He sailed for France. During the French Revolution, Bolívar looked to that country as an example of what Latin America could become. Revolutionary leader Napoleon Bonaparte, Bolívar thought, was going to set Europe up for an era of freedom and democracy. But once Napoleon declared himself emperor, Bolívar quickly lost all respect for him. Bolívar stayed in Europe until 1807, studying and soaking in revolutionary ideas. He returned to South

ROYAL RUNDOWN

➤ **BORN:** July 24, 1783, Caracas, Venezuela ➤ **DIED:** December 17, 1830, Santa Marta, Colombia
➤ **LED:** Venezuela, Bolivia, Colombia, Ecuador, and Peru ➤ **REMEMBERED FOR:** Playing a major role in freeing much of South America from Spanish rule

Painting depicting Simón Bolívar after battle (above); a statue of Bolívar atop his horse in Santo Domingo, Dominican Republic (left)

America determined to do whatever he could to help his people break away from the Spanish Empire.

FIGHT FOR FREEDOM

In a twist of fate, it was Napoleon who wound up providing the spark Bolívar and other revolutionaries needed after all. When Napoleon invaded Spain in 1808, he forced Spain's King Ferdinand VII to give up his throne and put his own brother on the throne of Spain instead. Bolívar and other South Americans looking for independence saw the change-up as an opportunity to finally claim their independence—and they were ready to fight for it.

Bolívar was often at the forefront of that fighting. He defeated Spanish forces and helped establish the First Republic of Venezuela in 1810, but then, Spain took over again. Bolívar refused to give up. He helped establish the Second and then the Third Republic of Venezuela. Bolívar also commanded forces that captured Bogotá, Colombia, after a brazen march over the Andes Mountains. From Panama to Peru, Bolívar was an active and accomplished military commander.

INDEPENDENCE AT LAST

Bolívar wasn't just brave on the battlefield—he was a talented ruler as well. He was briefly president of the Second and Third Republics of Venezuela, as well as president of Peru, Colombia, and Bolivia. Bolivia bears his name to this day. Bolívar hoped that he could persuade the peoples of South America to band together in a federation and become a united government, the way the revolutionaries up north had created the United States of America.

In the end, the countries of South America stayed separate. Bolívar's grand dream of a unified continent never came to pass. He died of tuberculosis in 1830, knowing that he had brought new liberties and new opportunities to his people. Today, he is celebrated as a genius revolutionary and hero of Latin America.

COMMANDING QUEENS

EXPANDER OF AN EMPIRE
Isabella I (1451–1504)

Without Queen Isabella I, there might be no Simón Bolívar: It was she who took Latin America under Spanish control in the first place. Isabella was one of history's most influential—and controversial—rulers. She united what had been warring kingdoms in her country into one mighty empire. Then she expanded her borders beyond Spain, sending Christopher Columbus west to find a sea route to India and Asia. Though Columbus didn't find India, he did find what came to be known as the West Indies—the gateway to the New World. That began the Spanish Empire's three-century-long control of the Caribbean islands and much of North and South America. Isabella made her nation into a world power, but it was at the expense of thousands of lives—not just those she conquered, but her own people's as well. Isabella's brutal Spanish Inquisition, established in 1478, hunted down and killed anyone deemed an enemy of her empire.

FACING **DEFEAT**

Kings Who Lost Their Kingdoms

Some royals rule with wisdom and justice. Others put their own wealth and glory ahead of the needs of those they rule, creating unrest and disarray. Either way, the will of discontented subjects can turn a once mighty empire into a shadow of its former self. These are rulers whose kingdoms suffered serious downsizing.

THE KING WHO LOST AMERICA:
George III (1738–1820)

Fearing revolt, British redcoats came to Concord, Massachusetts, to confiscate weapons from American colonists on April 19, 1775. During the confrontation, somebody fired what would come to be called "the shot heard around the world"—the first shot of the American Revolution. The following year, when leaders of the rebellion drafted a Declaration of Independence, they made sure to list how the colonies had suffered under the reign of the British king. That king was George III, the unlucky monarch who sat upon the throne when decades of American grievances came to a roaring boil. George was strongly opposed to the American bid for independence, even threatening to give up his crown when his troops were forced to surrender in 1781. In the end, George kept his kingship but lost some of Britain's most important colonies.

THE LAST MONARCH: Louis XVI (1754–1793)

Louis XVI ruled France as many kings had before him: with total power and word that was law. Unfortunately for Louis, he was also France's last absolute monarch. He ruled during the age of the Enlightenment, a period in which ideas like liberty and equality were becoming popular and ordinary citizens were revolting against their overbearing kings. France had just helped the British colonists in America break free from their king when the French people began clamoring for the same liberty. On July 14, 1789, after most of the country endured years of extreme poverty and starvation while Louis and his wife, Marie Antoinette (p. 53), lived in luxury, the French people stormed a fortress known as the Bastille. It was the beginning of the end. Louis was captured by his people and beheaded in 1793, sending shock waves throughout Europe. Suddenly, the young French republic was fighting wars with just about every nearby country. In the ensuing chaos, a general named Napoleon Bonaparte came to rule France as emperor.

HE PUT THE WORLD AT WAR:
Kaiser Wilhelm II (1859–1914)

Arrogant and hotheaded, Wilhelm II rose to power in 1888 as the German kaiser, or emperor, and the king of Prussia. Within two years, he had thrust Germany into political disarray by ousting the longtime power behind the throne, Chancellor Otto von Bismarck. Swaggering and quick-tempered, Wilhelm was obsessed with increasing the strength of Germany's military. He made foreign policy decisions based on his emotions, straining Germany's ties with other nations. He particularly offended the British people, publicly saying that the English were "mad as March hares." Then, on June 28, 1914, Archduke Franz Ferdinand, heir to the Austro-Hungarian Empire, was assassinated in Bosnia. Without considering the consequences of his actions, Wilhelm pledged German support for Austria. That set off a chain reaction, forcing Russia and its allies, France and Britain, to declare their opposition to Germany and Austria. It was the beginning of World War I, which would go on to cause the deaths of more than 18 million people. By 1918, Germany was on the brink of defeat and short on troops and materials after years of battle. The people called for the kaiser to abdicate his throne. On November 10, 1918, Wilhelm boarded a train to the Netherlands and spent the rest of his life there in exile, never again to return to the country he had brought to ruin.

THE LAST TSAR:
Nicholas II (1868–1918)

For 300 years the Romanov family ruled over Russia as absolute monarchs. By the time Nicholas Romanov II was crowned, in 1894, the Russian people had grown tired of being ignored; they craved a voice in their government. On January 22, 1905, a group of peaceful protesters marched to the Winter Palace to petition Nicholas for better working conditions. Tsar Nicholas ordered his army to fire on the crowd. The day became known as Bloody Sunday, which alone might have been enough to seal the monarch's fate, but from there he doubled down on disastrous policies, like inviting Rasputin—a mystic with a bad reputation—into his court, and personally leading Russia's armies in World War I into one defeat after another.

Then, in February of 1917, the Russian people revolted violently, and Nicholas II was arrested, forced to give up his throne, and executed. The Russian revolutionaries fought among themselves for five more years, ending with the rise of Vladimir Lenin, among the most infamous dictators of the 20th century.

COMMANDING QUEENS

FROM EMPIRE TO ALLIANCE
Elizabeth II (1926–)

In the aftermath of World War I, the British Empire had a presence on every inhabited continent. Much of Africa, the Middle East, and Southeast Asia was under British authority, as was all of India and Australia. British territory covered so much of the globe that people had a saying: "The sun never sets on the British Empire." But World War II left the British Empire battered and its economy devastated. One by one, the colonies began to slip out of the crown's control. India, which had been its most prized territory, gained independence in 1947. Over the next 30 years, Britain would lose nearly all its overseas holdings. But the reigning monarch, Queen Elizabeth II, was able to change with the times and turn what was once a mighty empire into an organization for the modern world: The Commonwealth of Nations, meant to foster trade and international relations, consists of 52 equal, independent countries—including India, Canada, and Australia—loosely associated by their ties to the former empire.

CHRISTIAN X

SYMBOL OF RESISTANCE

Between 1939 and 1945, Hitler marched his Nazi soldiers across Europe, bringing terror wherever he went. Country by country, the Nazis overthrew the leadership and claimed power. Many rulers fled, retreating elsewhere to keep themselves safe while they waited out the war. But Christian X of Denmark refused to act in fear.

When German troops occupied his country on April 9, 1940, Christian was forced to state in his official speeches that he would cooperate with the invaders. But meanwhile, he quietly showed his people that he had not abandoned them. Christian took daily rides on his horse through Copenhagen with no guard to protect him. The sight of their king, alone on his horse, became a symbol of independence and resistance to the Danish people.

During the first few years of the occupation, Jewish people in Denmark were not subjected to the horrors that they were in many other countries. But that changed in August of 1943, when German authorities took control of the Danish armed forces, and began making arrangements to deport Denmark's Jews to concentration camps. King Christian could no longer stay quiet. Though it put him in grave danger, Christian encouraged his people to disobey the Nazis. In response, thousands of Danish citizens launched a nationwide rescue effort. They hid their Jewish neighbors in their homes, smuggled them onto boats, and led them to safety in neutral Sweden.

Even after the Germans found, arrested, and deported several hundred Jews, the Danish people did not give up. They sent food and supplies to their countrymen and made constant demands to visit them, likely preventing many deaths. It was incredibly risky, but King Christian led his people to do what he knew was right.

Over the course of only about three weeks, the Danish people managed to ferry more than 7,000 of their Jewish fellow citizens to Sweden.

ROYAL RUNDOWN

BORN: September 26, 1870, Charlottenlund, Denmark   **DIED:** April 20, 1947, Copenhagen, Denmark   **LED:** Denmark   **REMEMBERED FOR:** Encouraging his citizens to protect thousands of Danish Jews from the Nazis

PEDRO II

I n the 1800s, most of Latin America was made up of republics and nation-states ruled by the people. There was one big exception: the empire of Brazil, which from 1882 to 1889 stretched across a huge territory where the countries of Brazil and Uruguay are today. Its second and final emperor, Pedro II, led Brazil to become a 19th-century world power. During the height of the empire of Brazil's glory, only the United States of America had a more robust economy in all of the Western Hemisphere.

But when Pedro II became emperor in 1841, it was on the verge of collapse. His father had left the throne when Pedro II was only five years old, heading to Lisbon to help his daughter claim the Portuguese throne. Pedro II was crowned emperor when he was just 16 years old. Even though he was young, he proved to be a capable ruler. Under his guidance, Brazil began producing coffee and constructing railroads and telegraph lines. The once weak economy flourished.

But despite the prosperity enjoyed by his people, one thing weighed heavily on Pedro's mind: slavery. More than half of Brazil's people were slaves. Pedro was one of the few Brazilians who wanted to abolish slavery. He knew the people who kept him in power, many elite landowners who depended on slaves to farm coffee, would be upset if he did anything to interfere with Brazil's slave system. Nevertheless, in 1888, Pedro outlawed slavery, freeing 700,000 men, women, and children.

That act, along with others (including a heated disagreement with the Catholic Church), was a severe blow to the emperor's popularity. On November 15, 1889, he was forced to step down from the throne, and he spent the rest of his life in exile in Europe. But during his reign, he had shaped Brazil into a successful, modern country, and the people of Brazil still celebrate his memory today.

Pedro II took a 10-month trip to Europe during which he traveled incognito, concealing his true identity and behaving more like a tourist than an emperor.

ROYAL RUNDOWN

➡ **BORN:** December 2, 1825, Rio de Janeiro, Brazil   ➡ **DIED:** December 5, 1891, Paris, France
➡ **LED:** Empire of Brazil   ➡ **REMEMBERED FOR:** Ushering in a modern era for Brazil

IN SHINING ARMOR

In the wars of yore, sturdy armor could be the difference between life and death—so kings who braved the battlefield usually wore the best armor available. Quality armor protected its wearer against multiple types of weapons while still allowing the movement necessary to engage the enemy. Check out some of the coolest armor that has been used to protect kings—and their soldiers—around the world.

ANIMAL ARMOR

Throughout history, some animals donned armor along with their soldiers, including battle horses and even dogs! But did you also know that elephants wore armor? War elephants, first used in about 1100 B.C. in what is now India, were sometimes equipped with elaborate sets of armor made of many connected metal plates. The garb could weigh more than 350 pounds (159 kg). Some were also adorned with "tusk swords," which were metal weapons mounted on the elephants' tusks, and others were saddled with carriages from which archers could fire on their enemies.

ARTFUL **ARMOR**

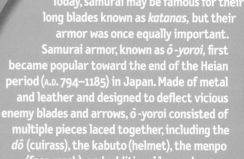

Today, samurai may be famous for their long blades known as *katanas*, but their armor was once equally important. Samurai armor, known as *ō-yoroi*, first became popular toward the end of the Heian period (A.D. 794–1185) in Japan. Made of metal and leather and designed to deflect vicious enemy blades and arrows, ō-yoroi consisted of multiple pieces laced together, including the *dō* (cuirass), the kabuto (helmet), the menpo (face mask), and additional leg and arm guards. The metal of ō-yoroi was covered in black lacquer to prevent rusting. Many dō and kabuto were decorated so intricately or made into such complex shapes that today ō-yoroi is regarded as art as much as armor!

SCALY **SAFETY**

During the Achaemenid Empire (550 B.C.–330 B.C.), stretching from what is now the Balkan Peninsula in southeast Europe to the Indus River Valley in what is now South Asia, Persian soldiers were so skilled—and so numerous—that their enemies called them "the Immortals." These valiant warriors likely wore scale armor, which was made of small metal pieces attached together over their brightly colored tunics. They also wore trousers, donned soft caps, and held large wooden shields. Horse riders covered their legs with scale armor and may have even had specialized armor for their horses! Together, the Immortals (and their colorful armor) terrified enemies far and wide.

FIERCE **FIGHTERS**

The Aztec Empire, which reigned over central Mexico from 1345 to 1521, was renowned for its fierce fighters. Some of the most elite of these warriors were the *ocēlōtl:* the jaguars. On top of the padded cotton armor worn into battle by most Aztec soldiers, jaguar warriors donned fearsome symbols of their namesakes. One such piece of armor was a wooden helmet shaped like a jaguar head, with room for the soldier to peek out from beneath the teeth. Rulers sometimes even wore capes made from jaguar pelts! These towering, brightly colored costumes were thought to transfer the abilities of the jaguar to the wearer and also likely caused enemy armies to turn tail and run.

CUMBERSOME **COVERINGS**

Though being a knight may sound exciting, wearing metal armor was decidedly less so. Plate armor, invented around the late 1300s, was heavy and offered poor visibility. However, since it was made of bands of steel over leather, it also defended its wearer against heavy blows while allowing for a decent amount of movement. Those wearing mail armor, which was made of interlocking metal circles often accompanied by a quilted fabric underlayer, were well protected against cuts from spears and arrows. The best protection? Probably a combination of both!

LORDS OF LEGEND

Some of history's most inspiring kings lived only in stories. These rulers of thousands of myths and tales from around the globe are an important part of the history and culture of many nations. Some may have been based on real-life leaders; others are entirely the stuff of fiction. But though their thrones are imaginary, their influence is not. While real kings can rule only for a lifetime, these legendary leaders' reigns have stood the test of time.

Actor Chadwick Boseman as
King T'Challa of Wakanda, also
known as superhero Black Panther

GILGAMESH

Ancient Sumer was one of the first great civilizations on Earth. The earliest known society in Mesopotamia, its citizens did all the things modern people do—grew their food on farms, built cities, and entertained each other with stories—but they were doing it as early as 5500 B.C. One Sumerian tale was so famous that it survives to this day: *The Epic of Gilgamesh*. It's a tale of a powerful king who went on a heroic quest to seek immortality.

DIVINE POWER

Gilgamesh's tale was originally written on 12 clay tablets between 2150 and 1400 B.C., discovered in the library of an ancient Assyrian king named Ashurbanipal. Together, they tell *The Epic of Gilgamesh,* perhaps the oldest written story on Earth. Though the tale is fictional, experts think the legendary Gilgamesh was probably based on a real-life king who ruled the kingdom of Uruk in southern Mesopotamia sometime in the 26th century B.C.

As the lore goes, Gilgamesh was two-thirds god and one-third man. His immortal blood made him unbeatable in battle, and he was famous far and wide as a great builder and warrior, and a knower of all things on land and sea. But his divine ancestry didn't make Gilgamesh a perfect leader: Eventually, all that power went to his head, and he began to rule the Sumerian city of Uruk as a tyrant.

> "Forget death and seek life!"
> —Gilgamesh

AN ANSWER TO PRAYERS

The people of Uruk begged the gods for help. Anu, a god of the sky, answered their cries. He created Enkidu, a wild man who lived among animals before he traveled to Uruk to take up city life. There, Enkidu and Gilgamesh clashed in an epic battle. For a while, it seemed like Enkidu was going to be able to match the awesome strength of Gilgamesh, but after a long one-on-one fight,

ROYAL RUNDOWN

➡ **LIVED:** ca 2700 B.C.   ➡ **RULED:** Uruk, Mesopotamia (in modern-day Iraq)
➡ **GREATEST FEAT:** Realizing his greatest purpose was his people

Illustration depicting Gilgamesh subduing two bulls (above); a weight with an engraving that shows Gilgamesh fighting two snakes, circa third millennium B.C. (left)

the god-king forced the beast-man to submit. Nevertheless, Gilgamesh was greatly impressed by Enkidu's strength, and when the fight was over, they became good friends.

Together, Gilgamesh and Enkidu went off on two great adventures. First, they slayed the gargantuan monster Humbaba, who lived in a forest and was feared far and wide. That displeased the Sumerian gods, who had created Enkidu to stop Gilgamesh and were upset that the two had instead become monster-fighting partners. So the gods sent an even more terrible beast, the Bull of Heaven, to stop them. But the daring duo slayed that monster, too. Finally, the gods sent them an enemy they could not stop through strength alone: They struck Enkidu with a terrible illness, and he died.

A HARD LESSON

Gilgamesh was both sad and frightened to see his mighty friend brought down so easily. The tragedy made him realize that he, too, would die someday. So Gilgamesh set out to find the secret to everlasting life. After a hard journey—chock-full of monsters that had to be defeated, of course—Gilgamesh met with an immortal man named Utnapishtim, who told him about a magic plant that would make him young again. Gilgamesh found the plant at the bottom of the sea, but on his return trip to Uruk, he lost the secret of immortality when a snake stole the magical plant from him.

The epic ends with the god-king standing outside of Uruk admiring its great walls. There, he had a realization: The city walls, which Gilgamesh had built himself, were his greatest accomplishment because they kept his people safe. After all this epic adventure, Gilgamesh finally understood that true immortality doesn't come from magic but from creating something good that will last long after we're gone. Because they created *The Epic of Gilgamesh*, the Sumerians live on, too.

COMMANDING QUEENS

THE GODDESS OF WAR
Ishtar

Ishtar was the most important female god in ancient Mesopotamia. She was the subject of poems composed more than 4,000 years ago, making her the oldest deity that's ever been written about. Ishtar was the goddess of love, worshipped by everyone from those who wanted to catch the eye of someone special to those who wanted to bring a family closer together. She was also the goddess of war, and on the battlefield, she was so terrifying that she made even the gods tremble in fear. The earliest records of Ishtar were written by Enheduanna—the world's first author known by name, a high priestess who lived around 2300 B.C. According to Enheduanna's poems, Ishtar was a goddess of opposites: birth and death, beauty and terror, love and war. People in the ancient world worshipped this complex and powerful figure for thousands of years.

FOUNDING
FIGURES

The First Rulers

Nearly every culture has a myth about its own creation. These stories often focus on legendary founders—exceptional people performing daring deeds to lay the foundation for a new civilization. Some are grounded in truth, but others are stories designed to give people a sense of pride in their heritage.

EASTER ISLAND: Hotu Matu'a

Few ancient people were as a good at navigating the open sea as the Polynesians of the Pacific. Around 1500 B.C., these intrepid travelers conquered the biggest ocean in the world in a search for islands they could live on. The most famous of all of these was Easter Island.

According to the legends of Rapa Nui—the Polynesian name for Easter Island—a man living on the island of Hiva once had a dream about a distant island, unknown to the Polynesian people. He told Hiva's king, Hotu Matu'a, about the dream. Hotu called for his canoe to be made ready, and he led a party of settlers to the place from the dream—where they indeed found a beautiful island. The people of Easter Island thrived there for centuries. Their unique culture led to the creation of the awe-inspiring *moai*, the giant statues carved about 3,500 years ago that still gaze out to sea today.

MAYA: Hunahpu & Xbalanque

One of the greatest civilizations in history, the Maya ruled Mesoamerica from 1800 B.C. to A.D. 900. They had many myths, but one of their most important was the story of the Hero Twins, Hunahpu and Xbalanque. The twins were great athletes, excelling at the Mesoamerican ball game, a real sport played by all major civilizations in ancient Mesoamerica. They were so great that the gods called them to the underworld to face the Death Lords in a life-or-death ball game.

The Hero Twins knew the Death Lords had a reputation for cheating, and sure enough, the first ball was covered in knives. In the end, the twins saw through every trick and trap. They won the game and killed the Death Lords. Then they returned to the surface and climbed into the sky, where they stayed until the end of time as the sun and the moon.

CHINA: Huangdi

Also known as the Yellow Emperor, Huangdi is the part-real, part-legendary father of all China. Beginning around 2700 B.C., Huangdi jump-started tribal China into one of the world's earliest civilizations, uniting the tribes of the Yellow River territory under a single mighty government.

Some tales describe Huangdi as a mythical figure: They say he had four faces that he used to gaze upon his kingdom in four different directions. A procession of animals followed him wherever he went, and when he died, he rose to the heavens upon the back of a dragon as all of his subjects looked on. But other tales depict him as a real emperor who, with the help of his advisers, brought innovations like mathematics and writing to China, along with wooden houses, boats, the wheel, the bow and arrow, and writing—in other words, everything people need to build a kingdom.

ROME: Romulus & Remus

Twin brothers Romulus and Remus were, at their birth, condemned to die by the king of Alba Longa, an ancient city in central Italy. The king feared that, because their mother was the daughter of the former king, the boys might one day rise up and take the throne from him. But the servant who was ordered to end the twins' lives couldn't bear to carry out his terrible task. Instead, he put them in a basket and sent them down the Tiber River.

When the basket ran aground, Romulus and Remus were discovered by a female wolf. Instead of gobbling them up, the wolf took care of the infant boys until they were adopted by a shepherd called Faustulus and his wife, who raised the twins as their own. When the boys grew to adulthood, they killed the king who had condemned them to die and returned the kingdom to their grandfather. Then they decided to build a new city on the spot where they had been saved as infants. But the brothers quarreled over which one of them would rule. In a fit of anger, Romulus killed Remus, taking ownership of the new city and naming it after himself: Rome.

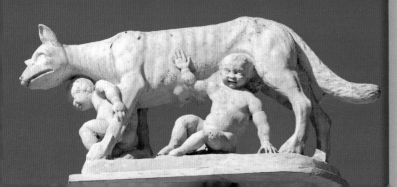

COMMANDING QUEENS

EMPRESS OF CALIFORNIA
Calafia

Long before the state of California was discovered, there was a myth about another California: a mythical island just off the coast ruled by a mighty warrior queen named Calafia. On the island lived beautiful and fierce black female fighters who wielded golden weapons and tamed wild griffins—mythical creatures with the body of a lion and the head and wings of an eagle. No men lived among them, and their ruler was the great Calafia. The myth of Calafia was created in the 1500s, when Spanish author Garci Rodríguez de Montalvo wrote about her in a tale called *The Adventures of Esplandián*. The tale was so popular that explorers like Hernán Cortés took it along on their first voyages to America. Today, the mythical queen is honored as the spirit of the state of California and has been depicted in artworks, stories, and films.

ARAGORN

═══ FULFILLING HIS DESTINY ═══►

Middle Earth, the land brought to life in the sprawling tale *The Lord of the Rings*, is full of dangers. Even around the relatively peaceful Shire, a stranger has been lurking. He's a scruffy, shifty character who seems more at home in the wilderness. But sometimes, greatness is hiding in the most unlikely of characters—a theme that runs throughout the *Lord of the Rings* trilogy.

The books were written by J. R. R. Tolkien, who was a professor of languages at Oxford University, in England, before he became a world-famous author. When he wasn't writing scholarly papers, Tolkien was penning something else: fantasy stories. Between the 1920s and the 1950s, when the series was finally published, Tolkien developed the trilogy that would come to be regarded as a masterpiece. And one of the most memorable characters he created was Aragorn.

> **"If by my life or death I can protect you, I will."**
> —*Aragorn*

A king without a kingdom, it's Aragorn's destiny to claim his crown. But the road to royalty is long and fraught with obstacles, and Aragorn becomes one of the major players in an epic battle of good versus evil that stretches through the series. Aragorn joins with eight others to form the Fellowship of the Ring to defeat the dark forces.

Through *The Lord of the Rings*, Aragorn faces down danger after danger, battling evil orcs, trolls, and goblins to protect his ragtag team as they set out to destroy a ring and save the world. In the end, he proves himself a true hero, deserving of his destiny: to sit upon the throne of his ancestors and rule as king.

ROYAL RUNDOWN

➤ **RULES:** Middle Earth ➤ **GREATEST FEAT:** Giving his all to save the world

T'CHALLA

King and superhero: T'Challa is both to the citizens of Wakanda, a fictional, technologically-advanced African kingdom. Star of Marvel comics, graphic novels, and the big screen, King T'Challa—aka Black Panther—battles foes both inside and outside his country to promote peace and ensure the safety and prosperity of his people.

Black Panther was the first African superhero to be the star of a mainstream American comic. Following his introduction in 1966 in Fantastic Four #52, the character made guest appearances in other comic heroes' stories. It wasn't until 1973 that Black Panther starred in his own comic book feature. And in 2018, the film *Black Panther* hit theaters to critical acclaim.

T'Challa is endowed with superstrength, heightened senses, speed, and agility after drinking the essence of Wakanda's heart-shaped herb. His kingdom also possesses a substance called vibranium. This fictional metal allows for scientific and technological advances—including Black Panther's energy-absorbing suit—unparalleled elsewhere in the world, and Wakanda goes to great lengths to protect it.

Wakanda may be science fiction, but it's based on a real-life African empire that reigned over much of southern Africa from the 15th to mid-18th centuries. Mutapa didn't have vibranium, but it did possess precious resources, including ivory, cotton, salt, and gold, that they traded with far-flung empires. The supreme king kept tight control over these resources, especially gold. The penalty for revealing a mine's location? Death! While the Mutapa kingdom seemed indestructible, it eventually fell after foreign invasions and infighting between chiefs led to a civil war—a downfall that T'Challa fights to keep from happening to his beloved Wakanda.

ROYAL RUNDOWN

➙ **RULES:** Wakanda ➙ **GREATEST FEAT:** Vanquishing evildoers and protecting his kingdom

"In times of crisis, the wise build bridges, while the foolish build barriers."
—*King T'Challa*

KINGS OF THE GODS

All-Powerful Rulers

In many cultures, there isn't just one god to worship—there are many. Ancient Egypt, for example, had more than 2,000 deities, including one that protected against snakes and another that kept people safe from nightmares! Much of the time, devotees would choose one god to rule the rest. Here are some of history's highest authorities.

MOUNTAINTOP MONARCH:
Zeus

As king of all the gods of Greece, Zeus sat atop Mount Olympus dispensing justice and controlling the weather. He was the god of sky and thunder, hurling lightning bolts down on Earth to keep the mortals in line. But Zeus wasn't always on top.

According to Greek lore, Zeus and his brothers and sisters were born from the Titans, beings who existed even before the gods. Fearing the new generation, Zeus's titanic father, Cronus, swallowed all his children. But Zeus survived—hidden from Cronus by his mother, Rhea. When he was fully grown into his powers, Zeus forced Cronus to release the other gods, then led them in a battle against the Titans that lasted for 10 years. Finally, the gods prevailed, and the Titans were locked away in the deepest pit of the underworld. This left Zeus with enough free time to become a father to Greece's greatest hero: Hercules.

WIZARDLIKE WANDERER:
Odin

Judging from the myths and legends they left behind, the Norse people weren't sure how to feel about Odin, the "Allfather" of the gods. He's often depicted as a wizardlike wanderer with a sweeping white beard and a wide-brimmed hat who uses a spear for a walking stick. Though he rules the gods, he often travels far from his home to visit the world of men on his own quests.

GOD OF CREATION: Amun-Ra

Sometimes depicted with the body of a man and the head of a falcon, the ancient Egyptian deity Amun-Ra was the supreme power in the universe. Legend says that he created the other gods and that humans sprang to life from his tears. Ancient Egypt's kings, called pharaohs, believed that Amun-Ra gave them the power to rule—so most of them tried to stay on his good side: The famous King Tut actually changed his name from Tutankhaten to Tutankhamun ("living image of Amun") to honor Amun-Ra. Egypt's capital was changed to Thebes, a city dedicated to Amun. And every year, pharaohs held a lavish celebration called the Opet festival. Priests carried a statue of Amun-Ra—dressed in fancy clothes and dripping with gold jewelry—from Karnak to Luxor, a 1.5-mile (2.4-km) journey. After they arrived, priests would perform a special ceremony to pray for a good harvest. The Opet festival also allowed people the rare chance to "talk" to the god: When a person would ask Amun-Ra a question, a priest—speaking from a secret spot within the temple's walls—would answer.

MASTER OF WEATHER: Indra

Nearly 4,000 years ago, people in what is now northern India practiced the Vedic religion. They worshipped many gods, but king among them was Indra, who sat upon a throne high in the heavens. A god of creation, he made the rivers and mountains, but his chief responsibility was weather.

Indra had gained the respect of gods and humans during a time of great drought. A massive demon-snake had come to sit around the world, blocking all the rivers and leaving fields cracked and barren. The serpent was so frightening that no one dared challenge it—no one except Indra. Armed with a thunderbolt, Indra fought the beast and blasted him back to the demon realm. The waters were released, and Indra returned to the sky where he aided the return of agriculture by sending rain on the world.

Over time, the Vedic religion was slowly replaced by Hinduism. By 500 B.C., the Hindu god Vishnu came to replace Indra as the most important deity, but Indra has remained an essential figure in the Hindu religion, as well as in Jainism and Buddhism.

Odin values wisdom so much that he once gave one of his eyes in exchange for it. He cares little, however, for justice or fairness. He's a god of poetry but also a god of war and death who rides across the battlefield on an eight-legged steed, with ravens representing thought and memory on his shoulders. From his throne, Odin observes all that occurs in the nine worlds of Norse mythology. And when his warriors are slain on the battlefield, it is Odin who meets them in Valhalla, or paradise.

A Viking wall hanging with a farming scene from late 12th-century Sweden

LEGENDARY SWORDS

HISTORY'S MOST FAMOUS BLADES

No storied warrior is complete without a mighty blade to wield. According to the legends, some contained unimaginable power and made their bearers unbeatable in battle. Others were so cursed it was decided they had to be destroyed. These are some of history's most well-known swords. Some were real, some were weapons of legend and lore, and still others were a little bit of both.

DURENDAL

ORIGINAL OWNER: Roland, faithful warrior in Charlemagne's (p. 22) army
LEGENDARY POWER: Stories say that a number of sacred Christian relics were forged right into Durendal, including St. Peter's tooth and part of St. Mary's robe. Durendal was said to be incredibly strong—able to hold back an army of 100,000. It was also said to be indestructible: When Roland thought all was lost in one battle, he tried to destroy the sword to keep it out of the hands of his enemies; instead, the powerful weapon blew a hole in the Pyrenees mountains.
CURRENT LOCATION: If Durendal ever existed, it's now probably lost. However, monks in Rocamadour, France, claimed that a sword stuck in the cliff above their chapel was the famed Durendal. That mysterious blade was donated to the Cluny Museum in Paris.

HONJO MASAMUNE

ORIGINAL OWNER: Goro Nyudo Masamune, master Japanese swordmaker
LEGENDARY POWER: Spanning from the mid-13th through the 14th centuries, the Kamakura period was Japan's golden age of swordmaking. The best swordsmith of them all was Goro Nyudo Masamune. Legend says the finest sword he ever crafted was the Honjo Masamune, which was named an official National Treasure of Japan.
CURRENT LOCATION: The Honjo Masamune was passed down through generations in the Tokugawa family, which ruled Japan for more than 250 years. But after World War II, Japan was forced to surrender its weapons—including samurai swords. The Honjo Masamune hasn't been seen since.

THE MURAMASAS

ORIGINAL OWNER: Muramasa Sengo, master Japanese swordmaker
LEGENDARY POWER: Muramasa Sengo was one of Japan's most famous swordsmiths, crafting blades during the Muromachi period, between the 14th and 16th centuries. As the legend has it, he was an expert at forging a blade, but he was also prone to bouts of violence. Muramasa passed on this trait to his swords, which would possess their owners, turning them vicious—just like Muramasa himself.
CURRENT LOCATION: The swords were popular in Japan until a rumor arose that they were cursed with the power to kill members of the Tokugawa family, which ruled Japan from 1600 to 1867. To protect themselves, the Tokugawas banned the blades, and many were melted down or had the marks on them changed to keep their origins secret. Today, it's difficult for experts to identify a true Muramasa.

THE SWORD IN THE STONE

ORIGINAL OWNER: Galgano Guidotti, a wealthy Italian knight
LEGENDARY POWER: Scholars think the fabled sword in the stone wielded by King Arthur is probably just that—a fable. But there is one real sword that shares a remarkably similar tale. The story says that knight Galgano Guidotti, born in 1148, experienced a divine vision in which the archangel Michael told him to renounce all his earthy possessions. Guidotti responded that this would be as difficult as splitting a stone, and he drove his blade into a rock to make his point. He was shocked when the sword actually pierced the stone.
CURRENT LOCATION: Beginning in 1185, a church, the Montesiepi Chapel, in Tuscany, was built up around the sword, still stuck in the stone. It's on display there to this day.

JOYEUSE

ORIGINAL OWNER: Charlemagne, first Holy Roman emperor
LEGENDARY POWER: Legend says the sword of Joyeuse took three years to forge, around the year 802 A.D. Meaning "joyous," the sword supposedly changed color 30 times a day and was so bright it could outshine the sun and blind enemies in battle.
CURRENT LOCATION: Joyeuse went missing after Charlemagne died, in 814 A.D. But in 1270, a sword bearing that name was used at the coronation ceremony of the French king Philip the Bold, and then for many kings after that. It was moved to Paris's Louvre Museum in 1793, after the French Revolution.

THE SEVEN-BRANCHED SWORD

ORIGINAL OWNER: Possibly Jingu, the legendary empress of Japan
LEGENDARY POWER: This sword is named for the projections that extend like branches from the central blade, all forged of iron. The branches make the sword delicate, and so it probably was designed to be a ceremonial rather than a military weapon. According to the gold inscription on the blade, the sword was a gift from the ancient kingdom of Baekje, located in modern-day Korea, to the ruler of Japan. Some scholars think that ruler was the legendary warrior-empress Jingu.
CURRENT LOCATION: Isonokami Shrine, Nara Prefecture, Japan

A reproduction of the
seven-branched sword

MINOS

I n 1900, an archaeologist named Sir Arthur Evans was excavating on the Greek island of Crete when he dug up the remains of a magnificent ancient city. Dubbed Knossos, it had huge palace complexes containing elegant paintings, jewelry, vases, and pottery. The finding confirmed historical accounts of a sophisticated civilization that had flourished in the Middle Bronze Age, from about 2000 until 1500 B.C. And the legendary ruler of this place was named King Minos.

MINOS AND THE MONSTER

According to Greek myth, King Minos was the son of Zeus, king of the gods (p. 76). Zeus fell in love with the beautiful mortal woman named Europa, and to make her fall for him in return, he used his divine powers to transform himself into a bull. With Europa on his back, the bull Zeus ran fast and then faster, taking off from the land and flying over the sea to Crete, where he changed back into his true form. There, in a cave on the highest mountain of Crete, Europa gave birth to three sons: Rhadamanthus, Sarpedon, and Minos. As princes of Crete, Minos and his brothers fought viciously over who would be king. Minos pleaded to his uncle, the sea god Poseidon, for help. Minos promised Poseidon that if he sent something from the sea, he would sacrifice it in his honor. And so Poseidon sent a pure white bull from the waters. It was so beautiful that Minos couldn't bring himself to fulfill his promise, so he sacrificed another bull in its place. But Poseidon saw through the trick and became angry. Poseidon caused Minos's wife, Pasiphae, to fall in love with the bull, and she gave birth to a terrible creature: the Minotaur.

According to one ancient text, King Minos was the first ancient ruler to build a navy.

ROYAL RUNDOWN

⇒→ **RULED:** Crete, an island in Greece ⇒→ **GREATEST FEAT:** Taking control of the throne of Crete

The Minotaur was half-human, half-bull, and all monster. It raged around the island until Minos constructed an enormous maze, or labyrinth, beneath his palace at Knossos and trapped the beast deep underground.

ROYAL JUSTICE

Around the same time, King Minos suffered a terrible tragedy: His son and heir, Androgeos, was killed by the people living in the nearby mainland city of Athens. Enraged, Minos took his navy, the most powerful in the region, and declared war on Athens, swiftly defeating the Athenians. Minos demanded that, for killing his son, Athens would submit an annual tribute of seven young men and seven young women to Crete. These tributes would be dropped into the labyrinth and fed to the Minotaur.

For many years, Athens faithfully sent their seven youths and seven maidens, delivering them on a ship with black sails to Crete. Then Theseus came along. Though he was the son of the king, Theseus volunteered himself as a tribute with the secret mission of ending the terrible tradition. When Theseus entered the maze, he carried a sword and a ball of twine, which he unwound as he made his way deeper and deeper into the maze until he finally found the great, hungry Minotaur. Theseus slayed the monster, then found his way back out by following the twine.

Minos died soon after. When he arrived in the underworld, instead of being judged for his misdeeds he was invited to continue to exercise his justice over Greece for all eternity by delivering judgments of the dead. Today, scholars believe that King Minos wasn't a real ruler but that instead the name Minos may have been used as a title for a series of kings who ruled Crete long ago.

THE MYSTERY OF THE MINOTAUR

How did the myth of the Minotaur come to be? Scientist Matt Kaplan, who investigates the intersection of myth and science, notes that all the myths about the Minotaur agree on two things: that the monster lived underground and that, when it roared, the earth shook. Shaking ground is something the inhabitants of Crete know all about. The island sits right on top of the fault line where two of the tectonic plates that make up Earth's outer shell collide. The area is so active that Crete can have more than 1,000 earthquakes a year! Kaplan points out that the myth of a ground-shaking monster could have been a way for ancient people to explain all those earthquakes. That makes sense when you consider a little-known fact about Poseidon, whose anger led to the creation of the Minotaur: Not only is he the god of the sea, but he's also the god of earthquakes!

MYTHICAL MONARCHS

Legendary Leaders From Around the World

People have told stories of rulers worth worshipping since the beginning of history. From a king who conquered a city with a giant horse to another known for his habit of making mischief, these divine deities were loved and feared for generations.

EMPEROR OF THE RIVERS:
Yu the Great

Chinese folklore says that Yu the Great, or Dayu, was the first king of the first dynasty in China because of the great service he did for his people. In Yu's time, around 2200 B.C., China was plagued by terrible floods; the Yellow River was especially cruel. Yu's father, Gun, tried to tame the waters by building a great earthen dam, but it eventually burst, causing some of the worst flooding China had ever seen. When he grew up, it was Yu's turn to try to stop the raging waters that smashed houses and devastated farmland. Yu built spillways and canals that carried the swollen rivers safely to the ocean. It is said that from the time he started his great project until the day he finished, he refused to set foot inside a house. It took him years of backbreaking work, but he tamed the floods and brought prosperity to the Chinese people, who then made Yu their king.

CLEVER LEADER: Agamemnon

A ferocious warrior and a viciously ambitious ruler, Agamemnon ruled the city of Mycenae in ancient Greece. He spent his days looking for a reason to go to war and increase his power. He got just the chance when his sister-in-law, the legendary beauty Helen, was kidnapped by the prince of Troy. Agamemnon assembled an invasion force, personally supplying 100 ships and set sail to get her back. Even with all his ships and troops of skilled fighters, Agamemnon couldn't get past the city walls of Troy by force. So he thought up a different, sneakier strategy: He gave the Trojans what they thought was a peace offering in the form of an enormous wooden horse. The Trojans took the gift into the city, and then that night, the squad of Greek soldiers hidden inside the horse slipped out and opened the city gates. Agamemnon and his men took the city and won the Trojan War that night.

CONQUEROR OF MONSTERS: Beowulf

The story of Beowulf is one of the oldest tales in the English language, written sometime around 700 A.D. It tells the legend of a monster-slayer and hero without equal named Beowulf, who journeys from his icy home in the fjord lands of southern Sweden to the shores of Denmark, where an evil monster has been attacking people and eating the king's soldiers every night for 12 years. Even though he is a stranger in these lands, Beowulf offers to kill the monster, Grendel. When the monster comes that night, Beowulf is waiting. After slaying the beast, Beowulf next bests the monster's mother, who comes looking to avenge her son. Beowulf returns to his home and is made king. His final act of bravery comes some 50 years later, when his kingdom is beset by a dragon. Once again, Beowulf defeats the beast, but this time is gravely injured and perishes shortly after the fight.

KING OF THE FAERIES: Oberon

Since the Dark Ages, the folklore of western Europe has whispered of a thin veil that separates our world from the world of the fae—the faerie folk, masters of mischief and magic. King among these otherworldly beings was Oberon. Like all faeries, he was a trickster, often giving gifts to mortal men—but those gifts came at a price. In one story, Oberon entered in the service of the French duke Huon of Bordeaux. Oberon gave Huon a horn, telling him he should blow it only in time of great need. But Huon blew the horn for fun—and found himself surrounded by 100,000 faerie warriors sent by Oberon to aid him. They were furious that there was no enemy to fight, and Huon nearly lost his life.

THE SNAKE GODDESS
Nu Gua

COMMANDING QUEENS

The earliest Chinese legends say that Nu Gua was the first human being and the first queen of China—a strong and independent goddess who created all of humankind. Her powers were seemingly infinite: When an enormous bull called the King of Oxen terrorized them, it was Nu Gua who controlled him with a magical rope and stopped the destruction. When the pillar supporting the heavens was damaged, it was Nu Gua who repaired it. She was also the patron saint of matchmakers and was responsible for all rules of conduct between husbands and wives. Ancient art depicts Nu Gua—whose heavenly palace later became the model for China's great walled cities—with a human head and the body of a snake.

SUN WUKONG

THE MONKEY KING

Sun Wukong was an imposter! According to Chinese myth, he was a supremely intelligent demon and shape-shifter whose only desire was to cause trouble. After being born from a magical stone egg, he lived among the apes on a peak called Flower-Fruit Mountain, and they crowned him the Monkey King.

The Monkey King lived a carefree life until the day he discovered mortality and realized that he, too, would die someday. Desperate to outwit his fate, he left the mountain to seek immortality. The Monkey King became a disciple of a Taoist master, and he gained magical powers like the ability to transform himself into whatever he wanted and fly thousands of miles in a single leap. But soon, the Monkey King grew too confident and began to challenge the gods. They sent the armies of heaven down to defeat him. But the powerful Sun Wukong was tricky. He fought when he could win and slipped away when he could not.

Every time he managed to escape, the Monkey King would sneak away on quests for magic weapons and armor—often stealing them from dragons. He had magical boots that allowed him to step from cloud to cloud and a shirt made of golden chain mail. But his favorite was a gold-banded staff called Ruyi Jingu Bang. It weighed more than eight tons (7.3 t) and could grow or shrink to any size Wukong wanted.

Despite all of Wukong's magic and his arsenal of super weapons, the gods eventually trapped him under a mountain. Even under its enormous weight, the Monkey King did not die; he remained there for 500 years, until a kindhearted monk named Xuan Zang came to his rescue. Wukong was forever grateful to the monk who set him free. He protected Xuan Zang on a pilgrimage journey, battling demons and monsters, and went on to become perhaps the most colorful character in Chinese literature.

> According to legend, the Monkey King could transform himself into 72 different creatures, including a tree, a bird, and an insect.

ROYAL RUNDOWN

➤ **RULED:** Chinese mythology ➤ **GREATEST FEAT:** Taking on the gods to declare himself king of the world

COYOTE

●─[===── NATIVE AMERICAN TRICKSTER ──===]──►

Hundreds of versions of stories featuring Coyote exist in the oral traditions of Native American peoples all across the continent of North America. In one story from the Salish people of the Pacific Northwest, Coyote was given a magic cow. So long as Coyote ate just a few bites of the magical cow, its flesh would grow back and he'd have food forever. But after a while, Coyote allowed his appetite to get the better of him: He killed the cow, thinking no one would ever know. But as soon as he began his feast, crows came and ate all the meat. Coyote was upset, but he consoled himself by thinking about the soup he could make from the bones.

As he started to prepare the soup, a woman saw him and told Coyote he was too important a figure to make his own soup; she offered to make it for him. Delighted, Coyote fell asleep dreaming about the meal he was about to eat. But when he woke up, the soup was gone and his pile of bones had been replaced by a pile of pine branches. Coyote could have had food forever, but he was left with nothing because of his greed.

Coyote was often so confident in his ability to fool others that he forgot that he, too, could be fooled. Sometimes Coyote is able to trick more powerful animals, but more often than not, Coyote stories are meant to instruct people in what *not* to do in life to be a better person. The lesson is this: Do like Coyote and you will get what's coming to you!

> In one legend, Coyote stole fire and gave it to humans as a gift.

ROYAL RUNDOWN

➤ **RULED:** Native American stories ➤ **GREATEST FEAT:** Teaching humankind about its greatest weaknesses

GODLY
GADGETS

In the cosmic battles of good versus evil, even the gods didn't show up empty-handed. Mythical leaders often wielded divine weapons with powers almost as awesome as their owners'. It's hard to imagine some of these heroes without their trusty tools—after all, what's Zeus without his lightning bolts, or Thor without his hammer? Read on to discover some of the most enchanted armaments from ancient myth.

HEROIC
HAMMER

You may have heard of Thor's hammer, Mjölnir (me-OLE-near). There's a reason for that: Mjölnir is really, *really* cool—essentially a super-powered cross between a guided missile and a boomerang. Once it's thrown, this hammer never misses its target. And then it returns right back to the hand that threw it. Mjölnir is only *nearly* perfect, thanks to its origin: Loki, the Norse trickster god, bet blacksmiths Brokkr and Sindri that they couldn't forge a war hammer as fine as those made by their rivals. Challenge accepted, they set to work on the perfect hammer. But before they could complete their weapon, Loki turned into a fly and bit Brokkr on the eyelid—blinding the blacksmith just long enough that he accidentally made the hammer's handle too short. Stubby handle aside, Mjölnir is still Thor's faithful sidekick—in Norse myth and Hollywood films, alike.

A 10th-century Viking amulet in the form of Thor's hammer, Mjölnir

MAJESTIC **MACE**

Sharur (or Car-ur) is a mythical mace, wielded by Ninurta, an ancient Babylonian rain god. A mace is a kind of special club with a big, heavy sphere on one end. Instead of the traditional sphere, Sharur's heavy end resembles a ferocious lion. Not impressed yet? There's more: This magical mace transforms into an actual living, breathing lion … that can fly. And talk. Legend says a demon named Asag once attacked the Babylonian gods with a powerful stone army. Ninurta sent Sharur to spy on the enemy forces from above and report back on their positions. With Sharur's intel, the gods bested the attacking army.

HELM OF **HADES**

Zeus shakes the heavens with his lightning bolts. Poseidon rules the seas with a powerful trident. And Hades … has a helmet. In ancient Greek mythology, Hades seems to get the short end of the stick when it comes to godly power. But there's more to his helmet than meets the eye. It can turn its wearer completely invisible—even to the gods themselves! For this reason, the helmet is also sometimes called the Cap of Invisibility or the Helm of Darkness. Hades isn't the only one who's benefited from the helm's powers, though. In one myth, the hero Perseus finds it. After he beheads the famous snake-haired Gorgon Medusa, Perseus uses the Helm of Hades to become invisible and escape the clutches of her Gorgon sisters.

CHAPTER FIVE

KINGS OF CREATIVITY

These rulers weren't real-life monarchs. But they were leaders all the same. In place of kingdoms, they led casts of actors. Instead of scepters, they wielded pens and paintbrushes. Through art, music, architecture, poetry—and even video games—they shook things up and gave us something to think about. In doing so, they changed the way people view the world. All of them reigned as kings of imagination—and inspired us along the way.

Elvis Presley performing on television in June 1968

LIN-MANUEL
MIRANDA

➤═ **MUSICAL MONARCH** ═╾•

New York City is famous for its skyscrapers and bustling business scene. It's the financial heart of the American economy, but it's also a melting pot where immigrants and their descendants have been blending their backgrounds since the founding of America. These cultural influences have found their way into New York's Metropolitan Museum of Art, Carnegie Hall, and, of course, the theaters of Broadway. It was in this diverse and creative place that Lin-Manuel Miranda became one of the world's foremost modern musicmakers.

A TASTE FOR THE STAGE

As a boy, Miranda was surrounded by music: His parents, both native Puerto Ricans, loved the songs of Broadway. Though they weren't often able to afford to see live performances, they listened to show recordings at home. And growing up in New York City in the '80s and '90s gave Miranda a front-row seat to new forms of music. Above all, he loved rap and hip-hop.

As an older kid, Miranda decided to try out theater for himself. He got involved in student-run stage productions throughout middle and high school and went on to study theater at Wesleyan University. There, he started writing his own musical, called *In the Heights*. It was set in the diverse Washington Heights neighborhood of New York City and blended freestyle rap and the Latin sounds of Miranda's ancestry with more traditional show tunes.

"I try to write shows where even the bad guy's got his reasons."
—Lin-Manuel Miranda

ROYAL RUNDOWN

➤ **BORN:** January 16, 1980, New York, New York, U.S.A. ➤ **LEADS:** The stage
➤ **KNOWN FOR:** Bringing the story of a Founding Father into the 21st century

NEW HEIGHTS

In the Heights debuted in 2008 and was a major success. It won a Grammy, several Tony Awards, and Drama Desk Awards, and was nominated for many more. All of a sudden, Miranda—who had funded his theater dreams by working as a substitute teacher—found himself catapulted to fame and the toast of Broadway.

Miranda worked on theater performances such as *Bring It On: The Musical*, lending his talent as a composer and lyricist. He appeared in TV shows, including *Modern Family* and *How I Met Your Mother*, and movies such as 2012's *The Odd Life of Timothy Green*. But Miranda's biggest career moment was set in motion when he went on vacation in 2008. It was then that Miranda picked up a 2004 biography of Founding Father Alexander Hamilton by author Ron Chernow. That might not sound like ideal vacation reading, but Miranda was engrossed. He started dreaming up a new kind of musical.

Miranda takes a curtain call after a performance of *In the Heights* (left) and performs a bit of *Hamilton* during the 70th Annual Tony Awards (above).

SHAKING THINGS UP

Hamilton hit Broadway in 2015, and it was unlike anything the theater world had ever seen. It told an old story about the beginning of America, but in a whole new way: The cast was young and multiracial. Debates about political policy played out in rap battles, ballads, and hip-hop. *Hamilton* made history feel fresh and modern.

It was a risky idea, but the risk paid off. Audiences went crazy for *Hamilton*. Ticket sales were through the roof, with everyone from schoolkids to then President Barack Obama filling sold-out theaters. In April 2016, the musical won the Pulitzer Prize for Drama, and it set a new record one month later when it was nominated for 16 Tony Awards, winning 11. Miranda himself, who acted the part of Hamilton when the show opened, won two of them.

Today, Miranda is one of the most beloved figures on Broadway—and beyond. He has written and sung songs for kids' shows such as *Sesame Street* and *The Magic School Bus Rides Again*. He's even written music for huge movies like Disney's *Moana* and *Star Wars: The Force Awakens*. Miranda has forever changed the way Americans think about music and theater. And he's just getting started.

COMMANDING QUEENS

ACTING QUEEN
Helen Mirren
(1945–)

She's most famous for her Oscar-winning 2006 performance as Queen Elizabeth II (pg. 63)—just one of six times she's played a queen over the years. But Helen Mirren isn't just a make-believe monarch: She's Hollywood royalty whose 50-year career on the stage and screen has made her one of the most revered actresses alive today. Mirren discovered her love for acting early on: when she went to an amateur production of William Shakespeare's *Hamlet* at age 13. By age 18, she was acting with a youth theater group. By her early 20s, Mirren was starring in stage productions, playing famous roles such as Lady Macbeth and Cleopatra. As time passed, Mirren's career only built up steam. She is one of only 22 actors in history to win the "Triple Crown" of acting—a Tony, Emmy, and Oscar. In 2003, real-life Queen Elizabeth II honored her with the title Dame Commander of the Order of the British Empire—the female equivalent of a knighthood.

KINGS OF THE
CONSOLE

Pioneers of Gaming

Utilizing pixels instead of paintbrushes, computer game designers wield their talent, technical skill, and creativity to craft fantastical worlds that keep players coming back for more. Their canvas might be virtual, but these creators are the real deal.

BLOCK BUSTER:
Alexey Pajitnov (1956–)

One of the most universally popular puzzlers in all of gaming is the 1984 runaway hit *Tetris*. The game is incredibly simple: Different configurations of four squares fall from the top of the screen, and players must rotate and maneuver the blocks to create a complete row before they reach the bottom. *Tetris* was invented by Alexey Pajitnov, a Russian living under the regime of the Soviet Union who had invented it to test the capabilities of the Electronika 60, a Soviet computer. It went way beyond that, becoming one of the most popular games ever. Today, it can be played on nearly every electronic device, from computers to graphing calculators. The game is so iconic that it's spawned its own psychological condition—the *Tetris* effect, named for people who spend so much time playing the game that they start to picture everything around them as a series of falling blocks!

MINECRAFT MONARCH:
Markus "Notch" Persson (1979–)

Imagine being dropped off in the middle of the wilderness with nothing but your wits to help you survive. This is the world of *Minecraft*. The game has almost no rules: Instead, players collect tools and resources and use them to build anything they can dream up. It's an unusual premise, but the game has become an international phenomenon and the second-best-selling game of all time. There's also an education version that teaches kids problem solving, critical thinking—even how to code. The man behind the mine is Markus Persson, though most know him by his online handle: Notch. A native of Sweden, Markus fell in love with computer programming as a kid. He got a job coding for a mobile gaming company, but on the side, he worked on his beloved hobby project, *Minecraft*. He released the game on indie platforms in 2009 and was shocked when it became an overnight sensation. In 2014, Persson sold his game and his company to Microsoft for $2.5 billion.

GAME CHANGER: Jerry Lawson (1940–2011)

When he was growing up as a teenager in Brooklyn, New York, U.S.A., Jerry Lawson earned money by repairing TVs. He found inspiration in role models like African-American scientist and inventor George Washington Carver and became one of the few black engineers of his day. In the 1970s, he moved to Silicon Valley, in California, U.S.A., where he became a member of the Homebrew Computer Club, an early computer hobbyist group. There, he exchanged ideas with other club members—including Apple computer founders Steve Wozniak and Steve Jobs!

But Lawson would go on to make his mark in another field: video games. Lawson made it possible to play video games at home. Before him, games were hardwired to the console that played them—usually in an arcade—meaning that each video game needed its own separate console. Gaming changed for good in 1976, when Lawson released the Fairchild Channel F, the first home video gaming system that could run a variety of different video games loaded onto cartridges. Lawson's breakthrough paved the way for modern home gaming systems, such as PlayStation, Nintendo, and Xbox.

SULTAN OF STRATEGY: Sid Meier (1954–)

What's the secret that separates a boring game from one you can't stop playing? If you ask Sid Meier, he'll tell you that good games ask players to make meaningful choices. With this philosophy, Meier has built a gaming empire. His first hit was *Sid Meier's Pirates!*, a game that put players in the virtual boots of a pirate captain, sailing the seven seas and having swashbuckling adventures. Meier's other games have put players in charge of railroads, Civil War battlefields, and spaceships. But Meier is most famous as the father of the Sid Meier's Civilization franchise, currently on its sixth installment of the main series with numerous spin-off games. To create those games, Meier followed his own advice to the max: The choices players make change the game's plot so dramatically that no two gamers experience the same story.

VIDEO GAME VISIONARY
Kim Swift (1983–)

COMMANDING QUEENS

Kim Swift thinks that toys aren't just for kids. One of the industry's brightest young superstars, Swift blew gamers away when she released *Portal* in 2007. The game sent players on an adventure that broke the rules of physics, forcing them to rack their brains to renegotiate their relationship with the physical world as they rip open interconnected holes in space. Her second release was no less mind-bending: *Quantum Conundrum* required players to reverse gravity, slow time, and enter something called "the fluffy dimension." Swift's work earned her a spot on *Forbes* magazine's "30 Under 30" list of young creators in 2012. And *Portal* is now part of the permanent collection at the Museum of Modern Art in New York City.

B. B. KING

KING OF THE BLUES

The blues is a uniquely American musical genre. Born out of the work songs and spiritual hymns sung by slaves on Southern plantations, it became the foundation of virtually all modern American music, from jazz to rock-and-roll to hip-hop. And one man ruled the blues for more than six decades. His name was B. B. King.

King, born Riley B. King, dropped out of school in 10th grade, earning a living picking cotton and singing gospel songs on street corners. After serving in the U.S. Army, he got a 10-minute spot as a radio disc jockey in Memphis, Tennessee. He took the name Blues Boy (B. B.) King, and by 1948, he had become so popular with his broadcast audience that he was a local star. King started making his own music, recording a string of hits beginning in 1949. He then went on tour, averaging more than 300 shows a year for the next 30 years.

One night during a performance, the venue King was playing in caught fire. He rushed outside with everyone else but then turned and ran back in to get his beloved guitar. Later, he learned that the fire had started when two men fighting over a woman named Lucille knocked over a lantern. From that day forward, B. B. King's guitars were always named Lucille.

King released more than 50 albums in his lifetime, making him one of the most prolific artists of his day. He was inducted into both the Blues Foundation Hall of Fame and, because the blues did so much to influence rock, the Rock & Roll Hall of Fame. In 2006, he was awarded the Presidential Medal of Freedom, America's highest civilian honor. King passed away in 2015, but his dedication to music ensured that the blues live on.

> "Blues is a tonic for whatever ails you. I could play the blues and then not be blue anymore."
> —B. B. King

ROYAL RUNDOWN

➤ **BORN:** September 16, 1925, Itta Bena, Mississippi, U.S.A. ➤ **DIED:** May 14, 2015, Las Vegas, Nevada, U.S.A.
➤ **LED:** The blues ➤ **REMEMBERED FOR:** More than 50 blues albums and a lasting influence on music

ELVIS PRESLEY

⊶═ KING OF ROCK-AND-ROLL ═➤

He's called "the King" for a reason. Elvis Presley blended blues and country, gospel and soul, in ways never seen before in America. Presley wasn't the first rock-and-roller, but he was the first to bring the new musical mash-up into the mainstream—and one of the most iconic figures in American history.

Born to working-class parents in a two-room house in Tupelo, Mississippi, Presley grew up listening to gospel singers in church. On his 11th birthday, his mother gave him his first guitar. When his family moved to Memphis, Tennessee, a couple years later, Presley started hanging around the city's blues legends, like B. B. King. He combined these influences, along with his country roots, into a unique sound.

Presley released his first single, "That's All Right," in 1954 and quickly became a teen icon. By 1956, he had signed with RCA Records; released his first number-one single, "Heartbreak Hotel," and his first number-one solo album, *Elvis*; and signed a movie contract with Paramount Pictures. Even though he was the biggest star in the nation, Presley still served in the U.S. Army from 1958 to 1960.

But Presley was so much more than a musician. From the stage, he could bring audiences to tears or whip them into frenzies. Many tried to dismiss him as untalented and a bad influence, but try as they might, nothing could stop the King from doing his thing. He starred in 33 movies and played sold-out shows all around the country. His appeal is so powerful that even now, 40 years after his death, Presley is still performing: There are more than 85,000 Elvis impersonators in the United States alone.

> "Truth is like the sun. You can shut it out for a time, but it ain't goin' away."
> —Elvis Presley

ROYAL RUNDOWN

➤ **BORN:** January 8, 1935, Tupelo, Mississippi, U.S.A. ➤ **DIED:** August 16, 1977, Memphis, Tennessee, U.S.A. ➤ **LED:** Rock-and-roll ➤ **REMEMBERED FOR:** A new set of rules for rock

RULERS OF
RHYTHM AND RHYME

Kings of Children's Literature

These poets weren't just beloved children's authors. These masters of verse came up with new ways of telling stories that captured their audience's attention and held it fast. Their works made kids laugh and cry, taught them about the ups and downs of life—and helped them learn to read at the same time.

WITTY WORDSMITH:
Dr. Seuss (1904–1991)

Theodor Seuss Geisel worked as an illustrator before he decided he'd like to write a children's book. That book, *And to Think That I Saw It on Mulberry Street,* was rejected by publishers 27 times before it finally hit the shelves in 1937, launching Seuss's career as an author. One of his most important moments happened in 1954, when *Life* magazine published a report that found children were having trouble learning to read because their books were too boring. In response, Seuss's publisher challenged him to write an entertaining children's book using fewer than 250 words. The result, *The Cat in the Hat,* has become one of the best-selling children's books of all time. All told, Seuss published more than 60 books that have sold more than 600 million copies worldwide. In 1984, he was awarded a special Pulitzer Prize for his life's work helping kids have fun while learning to read.

MASTER OF SMART SILLINESS:
Shel Silverstein (1930–1999)

Author and illustrator Shel Silverstein has a knack for introducing kids to creatures they wouldn't meet anywhere else—a Meehoo with an Exactlywatt, the Toilet Troll, and a boy who turns into a TV. Verses about these and other colorful characters fill poetry books like *Where the Sidewalk Ends, Every Thing on It, A Light in the Attic,* and *Falling Up.* His 1964 book *The Giving*

VOICE OF A MOVEMENT:
Langston Hughes (1902–1967)

In the early part of the 20th century, mainstream writers didn't pay much attention to the lives of black Americans. When they did, black characters were often written as stereotypes with no depth or dimension. Then Langston Hughes came along. Through his poetry and his prose, he wrote about the black experience in a way that shed light on the lives of real people. Hughes fought for justice and equality through his plays, novels, and poems. He became a founding father of the Harlem Renaissance—a movement during the early 1900s that celebrated African-American heritage through art, literature, and music—and fused the music of African-American people, jazz, and blues, with traditional verse to create powerful, dynamic works that people are still talking about today. Hughes also published a dozen children's books to get kids thinking about the tough issues of racism and discrimination.

PRINCE OF POETRY:
Kwame Alexander (1976–)

With a publisher for a father and an English teacher for a mother, Kwame Alexander grew up in a house full of books. He loved reading, but around fifth grade, he lost interest. When he discovered poetry, however, everything changed. He was enthralled by the way poems can capture enormous emotions in a few short lines. Alexander went on to become an author of books unique for their hip-hop-inspired rhythm. His most famous work, *The Crossover*, is a novel, but it's written in verse like a poem—and it got a lot of young people excited about the power of poetry. Many of his books have become best sellers, and some have gone on to win big awards, such as the Newbery Medal for children's literature.

Tree, an emotional story about the love between a tree and a boy, has been published in more than 30 languages and is often named one of the best children's books of all time. He's so famous for his popular writings that people sometimes forget that Silverstein wore a whole host of other hats: He was a playwright, a songwriter, and a singer, too. He won two Grammy awards—one for "A Boy Named Sue," a song made famous by legendary musician Johnny Cash.

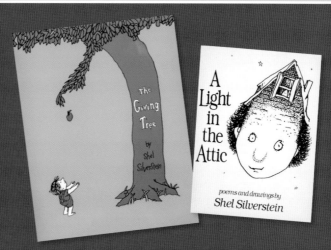

THE TEENAGERS
WHO INVENTED SUPERMAN

HOW TWO KIDS FROM CLEVELAND CREATED A COMIC BOOK SENSATION

THE ORIGIN OF THE MASTERMIND

The man behind the man of steel was a 17-year-old high schooler named Jerry Siegel. The son of Jewish immigrants from what's now Lithuania, Jerry grew up in Cleveland, Ohio, U.S.A., during the Great Depression. In June of 1932, Jerry's dad died defending his store from robbers. Six months later, Jerry had an idea: He sat down and created Superman. But the first Superman was a villain! And the first story he appeared in, "The Reign of the Superman," was published in Jerry's amateur sci-fi magazine, *Science Fiction*. Like Jerry, it wasn't terribly popular … yet.

ENTER THE ARTIST

Joe joined Jerry around age 10, when his parents, also Jewish immigrants, moved from Toronto, Canada, to Cleveland. After the two teamed up, Joe drew for Jerry's stories. The first Superman Joe drew was evil and bald—perhaps the inspiration for Lex Luthor, Superman's future arch nemesis.

A HERO IS BORN

In 1934, the comic book boys got a super idea! Jerry pitched a new plot for the Superman story, and Joe got to work drawing. In this new version, Superman was an alien infant set adrift by his parents to save his life. They gave him the tight blue suit, the flowing red cape, and the iconic *S* on the chest, and they sent him off to battle baddies and save the world. Before the United States had even entered World War II, Superman was battling Nazis with unmatched strength and speed, fighting for truth, justice, and the American way. Jerry and Joe also gave Superman a secret identity: mild-mannered Clark Kent, who mirrored the artists themselves. Like Clark Kent, Jerry and Joe were meek and wore glasses. But also like him, the boys held in their hands untold power!

THE SALE OF SUPERMAN

After working for years, Jerry and Joe finally found a publisher. In 1938, the Superman we all know and love made his debut in *Action Comics* No. 1. The two men wound up selling the rights to Superman to DC Comics for just $130. The pair battled DC Comics several times over the decades over royalties and ownership of the character, and while they never succeeded in reclaiming the rights to their creation, they did win a few settlements, including an annual stipend for life and the promise that their names would appear in the credits of all future Superman releases. Because of their fight, we'll never forget whom we have to thank for dreaming up one of the most beloved superheroes of all time.

FRANK GEHRY

═ ARISTOCRAT OF ARCHITECTURE ═╸⊶

With their swooping, billowing shapes, Frank Gehry's buildings seem to move across the landscape. One of the most famous architects of all time, Gehry has constructed groundbreaking structures all around the globe, often using unusual materials. In doing so, he's changed what people thought was possible in the world of architecture.

BUILDING-BY-NUMBERS

As a young man, Gehry had no idea what he wanted to be when he grew up. After his family immigrated to California from Canada in 1947, Gehry studied at Los Angeles City College. Meanwhile, he tried truck driving, radio announcing, and chemical engineering. But nothing stuck. So Gehry thought about what made him happy. He liked going to concerts and art exhibits, but he realized that, above all, what he enjoyed most about those outings were the buildings that housed those experiences. He was going to make those buildings.

Gehry earned his architecture degree from the University of Southern California in 1954 and began working. But he found the projects a little disappointing: His clients all wanted safe, boxy buildings. Because he needed to make a living, Gehry had to give his clients what they asked for—but he often didn't like what he created.

To make himself feel better, Gehry began to remodel his home in Santa Monica, California. He took an ordinary house and turned it into something dramatic—leaving the original conventional home intact and adding on a starkly contrasting modern addition in chain-link fence, sheets of glass, and corrugated metal. One day, a friend came to visit and asked him about the work he'd been doing on his house. As Gehry started explaining his design, it became clear to him that these kinds of structures were what he truly wanted to create.

> "I used to sketch—that's the way I thought out loud."
> —Frank Gehry

ROYAL RUNDOWN

⇒ **BORN:** February 28, 1929, Toronto, Canada ⇒ **LEADS:** Architecture
⇒ **KNOWN FOR:** Out-of-this-world buildings around the globe

BUILDING-BY-HEART

Gehry began to propose increasingly daring designs to his clients, and he was delighted to find that many people liked what he was doing. His new buildings were unusual, with bold and choppy segments and long, swelling curves. During this period, which started around 1992, Frank built the "Dancing House"—which looks like it is melting—in the city of Prague, capital of the Czech Republic. He constructed the striking series of metal arcs that make up the Walt Disney Concert Hall in Los Angeles. And he designed the Stata Center at the Massachusetts Institute of Technology, which seems to defy the forces of gravity.

To create his skyline-shaping designs, Gehry draws inspiration from everything from fish to sailing ships. He's a master at capturing the movement of these living things in his structures. He designs buildings with one goal in mind: to inspire emotion. And indeed, when 90-year-old veteran architect Philip Johnson stood inside Gehry's best-known building, the Guggenheim Museum in Bilbao, Spain, for the first time, the experience made him cry.

Some of Gehry's buildings include the Cleveland Clinic Lou Ruvo Center for Brain Health in Las Vegas, Nevada, U.S.A. (left); the Nationale-Nederlanden building (nicknamed the Dancing House) in Prague, Czech Republic (above); and the Guggenheim Museum, Bilbao, Spain (below).

COMMANDING QUEENS

QUEEN OF THE CURVE
Zaha Hadid (1950–2016)

The most successful female architect of all time, Zaha Hadid was a woman in a male-dominated field who had to fight her way to recognition. But she rose to the challenge and along the way earned the nickname "Queen of the Curve." Born in Baghdad, Iraq, Hadid moved to London at 22 to study architecture and design; her trademark became futuristic buildings with dramatic swooping shapes. Among her most famous creations are Michigan State University's Broad Art Museum, the Guangzhou Opera House in China, and the Aquatics Center for the 2012 Olympics in London. In 2004, Hadid became the first female architect in history to win the coveted Pritzker Prize, the highest honor in the field.

VISIONARY MASTERS

Art Outside the Lines

Some were painters, others were sculptors, and still others made creations that defied description. These artistic pioneers turned unexpected objects into their raw materials, created whole new styles, and, above all, made viewers around the world stop and stare in wonder.

KING OF CUBISM:
Pablo Picasso (1881–1973)

Pablo Picasso was born to be an artist: His first word was "piz," short for the Spanish word for "pencil." Picasso began formal training and drawing and painting at age seven. As a teenager, he would get in trouble at school and be sent to an empty room as punishment, but he loved it; he'd smuggle in a sketch pad and draw for hours. As he became renowned for his skill, Picasso began experimenting with radically different painting styles. One of his most famous was his blue period, when the artist, saddened over the death of a friend, painted almost exclusively in blue hues. Another was cubism, in which Picasso depicted people and objects broken apart, disconnected, and floating. This new movement inspired all kinds of new art styles, from futurism to art deco, and it's now regarded as one of the most influential art movements of the 20th century.

PAINTER WITH PURPOSE:
Jacob Lawrence (1917–2000)

Shortly after moving to New York City as a young teenager, Jacob Lawrence made a name for himself in the art schools of his Harlem neighborhood. He used blacks and browns set off by vivid colors to capture the spirit of his neighborhood. A master of observing everyday life, Lawrence became famous almost overnight in 1942, when he debuted his most famous work, the 60-panel "Migration Series" chronicling the historical movements of African Americans around the United States. When World War II broke out, Lawrence served in the U.S. Coast Guard as a ship's war artist and, afterward, painted his "War Series" to document his experience. He went on to create pieces for nonprofits including the NAACP Legal Defense and Education Fund, the Children's Defense Fund, and the Schomburg Center for Research in Black Culture. Lawrence is revered as one of the most important artists of the 20th century.

SINGULAR FIGURES:
Keith Haring (1958–1990)

Keith Haring loved to draw from the time he was a kid growing up in eastern Pennsylvania. He first learned cartooning skills from his father and from illustrators in popular culture, such as Dr. Seuss (p. 96) and Walt Disney. In 1978, he moved to New York City, where he enrolled in the School of Visual Arts and became part of a thriving community of artists creating innovative works outside of traditional galleries and museums. In 1980, seizing on an opportunity he saw in unused advertising panels in the city's subway stations, Haring began creating public drawings on them featuring his now-iconic graffiti-inspired figures. Over the next five years, Haring created hundreds of these drawings throughout the subway system—sometimes as many as 40 in one day! Throughout the 1980s, Haring won international acclaim; he was featured in more than 100 solo and group exhibitions and continued to create public artworks, many that benefited charities around the world.

RULER AND RULE BREAKER:
Felice Varini (1952–)

Kids are often told to color inside the lines. But Swiss artist Felice Varini doesn't even color on the canvas! Since 1979, he's been practicing an art form called anamorphosis, a special kind of painting in which he paints entire rooms, large open hallways, and occasionally entire city squares. But there's more to anamorphosis than just painting large areas: Varini's paintings look like a bunch of random shapes—unless they are viewed from just the right spot. Then they are enormous optical illusions that trick the brain into seeing massive floating objects in 3D space that aren't really there. One of his most incredible works is "Cercle et suite d'éclats," in which the artist created a series of perfect circles that seem to float in front of an entire village in the Swiss Alps.

COMMANDING QUEENS

QUEEN OF THE POLKA DOT
Yayoi Kusama (1929–)

She's one of the most famous living artists in the world. When she's due to have a new exhibition at a museum, tickets sell out months in advance, and lines can wind around the block. But the path to success was not easy: As a child, Japan-born Yayoi Kusama was plagued by hallucinations. The young Kusama coped by painting what she saw. Her visions of fields of dots became mirrored rooms that made the dotted objects inside seem to stretch to infinity. Just a couple years after beginning her career, she had sprung to the forefront of the male-dominated art world. Her works earned her the nickname "Queen of the Polka Dot" and led her to continue experimenting with mirrored "infinity rooms" that bring the viewer right inside her art. Kusama's work has inspired many other artists, including pop painter Andy Warhol.

GEORGE LUCAS

◄═══ LORD OF A GALAXY FAR, FAR AWAY ═══╾○

George Lucas didn't start out wanting to make movies; he planned on being a race-car driver. All through high school, Lucas dreamed of a life filled with high-octane hot rods. Then, just days before his high school graduation, he got into a wreck that nearly killed him. Fortunately, the Force was with him that day: Lucas lived on to write, produce, and direct some of the most famous films of the 20th century.

While studying cinematography at the University of Southern California, Lucas created a sci-fi student film called *Electronic Labyrinth: THX 1138 4EB*. The movie won him awards and a scholarship with Warner Brothers, where he got the chance to work with legendary director Francis Ford Coppola—a connection that helped George get started in the film industry. In 1971, he created Lucasfilm, a production company whose first release was a low-budget movie about being a teenager in the 1960s called *American Graffiti*. It was an Oscar phenomenon, earning five Academy Award nominations. All of a sudden, Lucas was a force to be reckoned with in Hollywood.

Now it was time for Lucas to fulfill his destiny by telling the story he had always wanted to tell ... the tale of comic strip superhero Flash Gordon. George loved the character and set out to make a Saturday-morning serial show for kids that would follow Flash Gordon on adventures in outer space. It never happened. Instead, the idea of charting the struggle between good and evil in galaxies far, far away evolved into a feature-film trilogy: Star Wars. When the first installment, *A New Hope*, hit theaters in 1977, audiences had never seen anything like it. People loved the captivating characters and were blown away by the special effects. The original trilogy is now considered a sci-fi classic, and altogether, the series has made more than $37 billion to date.

Lucas continued to dazzle audiences for decades with his rare combination of storytelling and special effects—including in the Indiana Jones series he co-created with fellow filmmaker Steven Spielberg.

> "Everybody has talent, it's just a matter of moving around until you've discovered what it is."
> —George Lucas

♔ ROYAL RUNDOWN

➤ **BORN:** May 14, 1944, Modesto, California, U.S.A. ➤ **LEADS:** Science fiction films ➤ **KNOWN FOR:** Creating *Star Wars*, a space opera that changed cinema

STEVEN SPIELBERG

⊷⟨═ STORYTELLER EXTRAORDINAIRE ═⟩➤

Today, he's one of the most famous film directors of the modern age. But as a kid, Steven Spielberg was bullied relentlessly. He was also already making home movies, spending hours after school writing scripts and editing film. So young Spielberg found a creative way to make his hobby the solution to his bully problem: He cast the meanest kid in a movie he was making about fighter pilots. The film was shot on a small handheld camera and used flour bags to mimic explosions. The bully loved the experience so much he never bothered Spielberg again.

Spielberg has never lost touch with what it feels like to be a kid. Many of his most famous movies, such as 1982's *E.T. the Extra-Terrestrial*, 1991's *Hook*, and 1993's *Jurassic Park* are now considered family classics. Along with fellow director George Lucas, he co-created the Indiana Jones series, about an adventure-seeking archaeologist. In the 1990s, Spielberg even produced seven cartoons for television, including the instant classics *Tiny Toon Adventures* and *Animaniacs*. His cartoons were famous for being educational and silly at the same time.

Not all of Spielberg's films are just for fun. He probed one of humankind's deepest fears—sharks—with 1975's *Jaws*. He explored what might happen if aliens landed with 1977's *Close Encounters of the Third Kind*. And he's made movies about difficult topics like the Holocaust and soldiers in World War II, too.

But Spielberg still has an ability to look at the world through a kid's wide eyes. In 2016, he released *The BFG*, an adaptation of a book by Roald Dahl about a big friendly giant and the little girl he befriends. And in 2018, he produced and directed the film *Ready Player One*, a sci-fi thriller set in a virtual-reality-based future. Today, Spielberg is a father of seven kids who are now adults, and he spends his days dreaming up stories that his grandchildren will love.

"I feel there is no substitute for going out to the movies. There is nothing like it."
—*Steven Spielberg*

ROYAL RUNDOWN

➤→ **BORN:** December 18, 1946, Cincinnati, Ohio, U.S.A ➤→ **LEADS:** From the director's chair ➤→ **KNOWN FOR:** An impressive body of modern film classics

AND THE OSCAR GOES TO ...

FIT FOR A KING

It might be smaller than most scepters or swords, but for kings of the screen, the golden Oscar statuette is about as good as it gets. Standing just 13.5 inches (35 cm) high and weighing a surprising 8.5 pounds (3.9 kg), the Academy Award of Merit—better known by its nickname, the Oscar—has been awarded to big-screen standouts since 1929. Here are some of film history's most marvelous men.

1950: JOSÉ FERRER

Born in Puerto Rico in 1912, José Ferrer graduated from Princeton University and had hopes of becoming an architect. Little did he know that he would soon be starring on Broadway! After almost a decade of success on the stage, Ferrer made the transition to film in 1948. Just three years later, he received the Oscar for best actor for his role in Cyrano de Bergerac, an adventurous romance about a swordsman in 17th-century France. Ferrer was the first Latino actor to win an Academy Award.

1964: SIDNEY POITIER

Despite growing up amid poverty and racial discrimination, Sidney Poitier was determined to follow his dreams. Born to Jamaican parents in 1924, Poitier's first attempts to join the theater were met with rejection—largely due to his heavy accent. But he never gave up, and by the 1950s he was appearing both on Broadway and in films. Poitier refused to accept the offensively stereotypical roles that were primarily offered to black people at the time and, in doing so, paved the way for many black actors and actresses who came after him. His talent and passion were undeniable; Poitier made history as the first black actor to win the Oscar for Best Actor for his role in the comedic drama Lilies of the Field.

2002:
HAYAO MIYAZAKI

Hayao Miyazaki was born in Tokyo, Japan, in 1941. He began his animation career at a young age in 1963 and proceeded to delight audiences with TV series such as *Future Boy Conan* and several successful films. He also began a career as a critically acclaimed manga artist and co-founded a renowned film and animation studio, Studio Ghibli. Miyazaki's talent has long been celebrated in Japan, where he received an award for best film for his 1997 movie *Princess Mononoke*. In 2002, his success was further recognized in America, when he became the first Asian ever to be nominated for—and win—the Oscar for best animated feature. He won for the fantastical coming-of-age film *Spirited Away*.

1972:
CHARLIE CHAPLIN

Born in 1889, Charlie Chaplin is perhaps best known for his mustachioed, bowler-hat-wearing, silent character known as the "Little Tramp." The Tramp first debuted in 1914 to huge success, famous for his silly walk, unpredictable antics, and charming ability to get out of trouble. Chaplin himself went on to star in many more silent films, shaping the future of film with his talent for slapstick comedy and improvisation. Chaplin's contribution to film was so enormous that in 1972, he was presented with an honorary Oscar for his remarkable talents and effect on the entire industry. When Chaplin accepted the award, the audience gave him a standing ovation that lasted for 12 minutes.

OF ALL TIME:
WALT DISNEY

It may come as no surprise that the person to be nominated for—and win—the highest number of Oscars is none other than Walt Disney. Born in 1901, Walter Disney began animating at a young age when he won a scholarship to the Kansas City Art Institute. He journeyed to Hollywood to try his luck in 1923, but it wasn't until 1928 that he created the world-famous Mickey Mouse (then known as Mortimer Mouse). Today, Disney's creations have inspired countless TV shows, films, theme parks, and more. So how many Oscars did the master have to show for his efforts? A whopping 32! He was nominated a total of 59 times.

1970:
GEORGE C. SCOTT

For many people, winning an Oscar is a lifelong dream. But actor George C. Scott viewed it quite differently! Scott, who was born in 1927, began acting in college. Over the years, he received nominations for roles as a supporting actor in various films. However, he wanted nothing to do with these nominations…or the Oscars! Scott felt that pitting actors against one another went against the principles of art and acting. And he was true to his word: When Scott won the award for best actor in 1970 for his role in the WWII drama *Patton*, he became the first actor ever to decline an Oscar.

Goldie Hawn presents Frank McCarthy with the Best Actor Oscar. McCarthy accepted the award on behalf of George C. Scott..

CHAPTER SIX

ARISTOCRATS OF **ACTION**

Most kings rule a kingdom, but these monarchs are a little different. From real-life athletes to cinematic action heroes, they put mind over matter to rule the track, the court, or the screen. It took these sovereigns of sport a lot of guts, hard work, and the right attitude to claim their place in this chapter. Some led teams to victory; others set records that still stand today. These are the stories of the crowning achievements of some of recent history's biggest winners.

Climber and photographer Jimmy
Chin on assignment in Yosemite
National Park, California, U.S.A.

BABE RUTH

THE SULTAN OF SWAT

Baseball icon Babe Ruth, born George Herman Ruth, Jr., was a rowdy kid who hung out in the rough part of town and was always in trouble. When he was seven years old, he became too much for his parents to handle. His father took him to St. Mary's Industrial School for Boys, a center for wayward children, and it became Ruth's home for the next 12 years. There, Ruth trained to be a tailor (he later liked to show off his sewing skills to his teammates). But most importantly, it was there that young Ruth was introduced to baseball, a sport that would change his life—and that he would change in return.

THE BIG LEAGUES

It was clear to all who watched him that Ruth was an exceptionally talented baseball player. By the time he was a teenager, he could play every position better than anyone else at his school—even catcher, despite the fact that the left-handed Ruth had to use a right-handed mitt. He was built to be an athlete, too, standing more than six feet (1.8 m) tall and weighing nearly 200 pounds (91 kg).

In 1914, a scout for the Baltimore Orioles—then a minor league team—recruited him to the team as a pitcher. Nineteen-year-old Ruth boarded a train to Fayetteville, North Carolina, U.S.A., where the team did spring training. It was the first time he had been on a train, left Maryland, seen the countryside, or ordered from a menu. With his first paycheck, he bought a bicycle. He was so young and innocent that his new teammates called him "Babe." The nickname stuck.

> "Never let the fear of striking out get in your way."
> —Babe Ruth

AMERICA'S GAME

At the time when Ruth was coming up in the sport, Americans were baseball-crazy. Television hadn't yet been invented, so for some big games, people would crowd into theaters to watch

ROYAL RUNDOWN

➨ **BORN:** February 6, 1895, Baltimore, Maryland, U.S.A.   ➨ **DIED:** August 16, 1948, New York, New York, U.S.A.
➨ **LED:** Baseball   ➨ **REMEMBERED FOR:** Being one of the best players in the history of baseball

people act out the play-by-play with an invisible ball. Ruth was the star who came along just at the right time.

He might have been new to baseball, but Ruth proved himself so quickly that, four months after leaving St. Mary's, he was called up to join the Boston Red Sox. The first major league game he ever saw was also the first one he played in. Over the next five years, Ruth led the Red Sox to three championships. A first-rate pitcher, he pitched 13 scoreless innings in one World Series game. And no one had even discovered his true talent yet: batting.

KING OF THE SWING

In 1919, Ruth was traded to the New York Yankees—beginning the "Curse of the Bambino," an unlucky streak in which the Red Sox didn't win another World Series for 85 years, until 2004. With Ruth on the team, now as a star batter, the Yankees won four World Series titles over the next 15 seasons. Ruth set record after record: In 1920, his first year on the team, he hit 54 home runs. In 1927, he hit 60—a record that stood for 34 years. Yankee Stadium, built in 1923, was dubbed the "House That Ruth Built." Over his career, Ruth hit 714 home runs. To this day, Ruth is one of only three players who have topped 700.

Ruth died of cancer at the age of 53. During his short life, he had shaped America's favorite pastime into what it is today. Even now, players still mimic one of his most famous moments: On October 1, 1932, in the fifth inning of game three of the World Series against the Chicago Cubs, Babe Ruth stepped up to the plate and pointed toward center field—directly at the spot where he proceeded to smack a ball 440 feet (134 m) deep into the center-field bleachers.

COMMANDING QUEENS

QUEEN OF THE MOUND
Jackie Mitchell (1913–1987)

The story is almost unknown to baseball lore. But on April 2, 1931, a 17-year-old girl pitched against the New York Yankees, striking out both Babe Ruth and Lou Gehrig—the best hitters ever to swing a bat. Her name was Jackie Mitchell.

In 1931, Mitchell—who had grown up playing ball in Memphis, Tennessee—was playing for a men's minor league team called the Lookouts, when a promoter known for his publicity stunts booked the team to play two exhibition games against the Yankees. It is believed to be one of the first professional baseball contracts a woman ever signed. The idea of a 17-year-old girl facing off against icons attracted a lot of attention. On game day, Mitchell stepped up to the mound, wound up, and struck out Ruth, then Gehrig. To this day, no one is sure what really happened. Did Ruth and Gehrig strike out on purpose to go along with the stunt—or did a young girl really strike out the mighty Yankees?

KINGS OF THE
SILVER SCREEN

Heroes On and Off Camera

From superheroes to sci-fi epics, the superstars on these pages know how to bring the action. These powerhouse professionals perform dazzling physical feats to deliver the perfect performance.

ZERO TO HERO: Chris Pratt (1979–)

Chris Pratt's big break into the movies sounds like the plot of a movie itself: While waiting tables, he chanced upon a movie star who wound up flying him to Hollywood to act in a film role. That movie was never released, but it gave Pratt a foot in the door. He landed in the national spotlight with the hit series *Parks and Recreation,* where he played the lovable, dimwitted Andy Dwyer. Pratt had always wanted to play an action hero, but first he knew he had to get into action hero shape. He began a training regimen that had him working out six times a week for six months. It took a tremendous effort, but Pratt stuck with it—and since then, he's become a bona fide action hero: fighting his way across distant planets in *Guardians of the Galaxy* (Vol. 1 and 2) and wrangling velociraptors in the Jurassic World movies. When he's not busy saving the world on set, he does it in real life, too: Pratt routinely visits children's hospitals and uses his celebrity to raise money for all kinds of charitable causes.

SCI-FI STAR: John Boyega (1992–)

John Boyega was warned. When he was offered the role of Finn, the renegade Stormtrooper turned Resistance hero in the Star Wars series, director J. J. Abrams cautioned him that shooting the latest trilogy would mean devoting a significant part of his young life to the epic franchise. But nothing was going to stop Boyega from accepting the role of a lifetime. He had been waiting for that moment since his first acting role, when he played a leopard in an elementary school play. The son of Nigerian immigrants, Boyega grew up in a public housing project in London, England. Now he rules the galaxy as Finn, and he's eager to share what stardom has brought him. Boyega founded a production company, UpperRoom Entertainment, and plans to use it to create more opportunities for black actors and foster diversity in Hollywood.

KNOCKOUT KING: Dwayne Johnson (1972–)

From pro wrestling icon to movie star to ... president of the United States? It's a long shot, but that could be the life story of Hollywood action hero Dwayne Johnson. Johnson began his stint in show biz as pro wrestling phenomenon the Rock. From there, Johnson traded spandex for the silver screen, taking on roles for which he could flex his mighty muscles, like the Scorpion King and Hercules. He's also shown an ability to flex his heart muscles, playing kid-friendly roles in *Jumanji* and *Moana*. For a time, he was the highest-paid actor in Hollywood. Johnson puts that money to good use in his charity, the Rock Foundation, which helps terminally ill children live their lives to the fullest. More recently, Johnson has expressed interest in running for president of the United States. Ever upbeat, charismatic, and optimistic, this monarch of muscle could be a leader in politics someday.

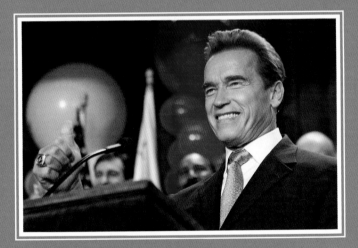

FROM TERMINATOR TO GOVERNOR: Arnold Schwarzenegger (1947–)

No chronicle of Hollywood's heavy-hitting kings would be complete without Arnold Schwarzenegger. By the time he came to America from Austria in 1968, he was already a world-famous bodybuilder. He won the Mr. Universe competition when he was only 20 years old. In 1982, he immortalized his muscles on the big screen in the movie *Conan the Barbarian*. Two years later, he took on his most famous film role, as America's favorite cyborg in *The Terminator*. In 2003, Arnold decided to become a real-life leading man: He was elected governor by the people of California and served the state for seven years. As a leader, he was committed to helping businesses thrive while also promoting policies to protect the planet from greenhouse gases. Since holding the highest office in California, Arnold spends much of his time giving back, promoting physical fitness to America's youth.

COMMANDING QUEENS

SCREEN QUEEN
Jennifer Lawrence (1990–)

Jennifer Lawrence has taken Hollywood by storm and has had fun doing it. Lawrence first captured America's attention as Katniss Everdeen, hero of the popular Hunger Games movies. She also revamped the Marvel villain Mystique in the ongoing X-Men franchise. And Lawrence has proved that she has acting skills—not just action skills. She's been nominated for four Academy Awards, winning best actress in 2013. Determined to emulate the heroes she portrays on-screen, the actress is heavily involved in giving back. She established the Jennifer Lawrence Foundation, which works with a number of charities that focus on a range of issues, from supporting after-school programs for kids to stomping out deadly diseases.

BRUCE LEE

MONARCH OF MARTIAL ARTS

Name any modern action flick with a fight scene, and it most likely owes inspiration to martial arts movie master Bruce Lee. He was born in San Francisco, but soon after, his family moved to Hong Kong, where his father was an opera singer. There, Lee got caught up in a street gang. He began studying the Wing Chun style of martial arts, but his improved fighting skills just landed him in more trouble.

Lee moved back to the United States at 18 to get away from his violent past in Hong Kong. He studied philosophy in college, then opened his own kung fu school, where he taught a new style of fighting that he himself invented. Jeet Kune Do, or the Way of the Intercepting Fist, is a martial art form that relies on counterattack—in other words, it is less for offense and more for self-defense. It also happens to look good on camera!

> "I fear not the man who has practiced 10,000 kicks once, but I fear the man who has practiced one kick 10,000 times."
> —Bruce Lee

Lee got a TV job on a 1960s live-action superhero show in which he played Kato, sidekick to the superhero the Green Hornet. Audiences were captivated by Lee's amazing moves, and soon he was more popular than the show's star. From there, Lee went flying into the films that made him a household name, including *Fists of Fury* in 1972 and *Enter the Dragon* in 1973.

Unfortunately, Lee died suddenly before *Enter the Dragon* made it to theaters. Though he never got to enjoy the height of his popularity, his legacy has proved to be as unbeatable as the man himself. The Bruce Lee Foundation's Little Dragons program teaches martial arts to at-risk kids. It doesn't just pass on fighting skills; it also imparts Lee's philosophy of confidence, personal responsibility, and personal greatness.

ROYAL RUNDOWN

➤ **BORN:** November 27, 1940, San Francisco, California, U.S.A. ➤ **DIED:** July 20, 1973, Hong Kong, China ➤ **LED:** Martial arts movies ➤ **REMEMBERED FOR:** Jeet Kune Do and two popular films

SUGAR RAY LEONARD

➤—⟨ KING OF THE RING ⟩⟶

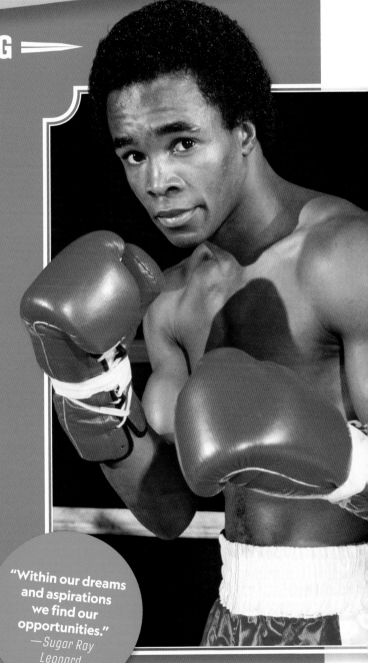

"Sugar" Ray Leonard is among the greatest—and most beloved—boxers in history. But growing up, he had little interest in sports. That changed on the day Leonard's brother, Roger, convinced their local recreation center to start a boxing team. From the moment Leonard put on his gloves, he was hooked. He had never liked team sports, but boxing was different.

There was no boxing ring in the area, so Leonard learned the sport on a basketball court. He became obsessed, practicing every chance he got. By the time he was 16, he was competing on the amateur circuit. He was good, but he had no idea how good until he won a match against a fighter who was trying out for the 1972 U.S. Olympic boxing team. Leonard's defeated competitor told him he should try out, too.

Although Leonard didn't make it onto the '72 team, he spent the next four years fighting harder than ever. When the next tryouts came around, he was ready. Despite battling hand injuries, he took home a gold medal at the 1976 Olympic Games in Montreal, Canada, becoming a household name along the way.

Leonard hoped to support himself with his newfound celebrity and retire from the sport. But shortly after the games, both his parents fell ill. Leonard decided that the best way he could help his family was to earn a living as a professional boxer—even though it meant giving up a college scholarship and having to subject his already aching hands to more punishment. He won title after title and competed in some of the sport's most historic matches. After finally retiring for good, in 1997, Leonard decided to fight another kind of fight. In 1999, he and his wife Bernadette started the Sugar Ray Leonard Foundation, which helps battle juvenile diabetes.

"Within our dreams and aspirations we find our opportunities."
—Sugar Ray Leonard

ROYAL RUNDOWN

➤➤ **BORN:** May 17, 1956, Rocky Mount, North Carolina, U.S.A.   ➤➤ **LED:** Boxing

➤➤ **KNOWN FOR:** An Olympic gold medal and 36 wins in 40 pro fights

GAME CHANGERS

Behind-the-Scenes Kings

It's hard to imagine a world before some of our favorite sports and pastimes. But believe it or not, all had to be invented, refined, and popularized. These game changers are responsible for some of the most beloved sports today.

BARON OF BASKETBALL:
James Naismith (1861–1939)

Winters in Massachusetts, U.S.A., can be brutal. Ice, wind, and snow can bring entire cities to a halt—so you can forget about playing sports outside! During a cold December in 1891, James Naismith, a physical education instructor at the International YMCA Training School in Springfield, Massachusetts, was looking for a way to keep his track-and-field runners in shape while they were stuck indoors. In a flash of inspiration, Naismith nailed two peach baskets to the gymnasium wall, grabbed a soccer ball, and invented a new sport: basketball. At first, the pace of play was slow. Nobody thought to cut holes in the bottoms of the baskets until 1912, so every time a player scored, the team had to stand around while someone fetched a ladder to retrieve the ball. But basketball really took off in the 1980s, when superstar players like Magic Johnson and Michael Jordan made audiences gasp with their dribbling and dunking—and fans haven't stopped cheering since.

INVENTOR OF ROLLER SKATES:
Joseph Merlin (1735–1803)

Not every story of a new sport was a rousing success. Joseph Merlin, born in Belgium in 1735, was an inventor and a craftsman of precision engineering; he built clockwork and musical instruments and introduced an early concept for a wheelchair. He was also a musician who loved to play the violin.

PIONEER OF THE GRIDIRON:
Walter Camp (1859–1925)

Before the 1800s, American football was more of a wild free-for-all than an organized sport. There were no limits on the number of players allowed on the field and almost no rules about what those players could do to move the ball toward the goal posts.

Even so, when he was a teenager, Walter Camp saw kids playing football and had to try it for himself. He liked the sport so much that he became a player, then a coach—first at Yale, then at Stanford University. For 48 years, he helped restructure the game and write the official rules. Camp's major contributions included assigning point values to touchdowns, field goals, and safeties. He also added lines to the field and came up with the idea that the offense had to surrender the ball if they didn't advance a certain number of yards after multiple downs. Today, Walter Camp's sport continues to evolve. New rules are continually added to make the game more fair, safe, and enjoyable for players and fans alike.

FATHER OF BASEBALL:
Doc Adams (1814–1899)

For years, people celebrated a man named Alexander Cartwright as the person who invented baseball in 1860. But in 2016, a groundbreaking discovery was made: a set of documents called "Laws of Base Ball" that outline the modern rules of America's favorite pastime, penned in 1857 by Daniel Lucius Adams.

Like many sports of the 19th century, the rules of baseball-like sports varied from team to team, city to city. Daniel Lucius "Doc" Adams, who got his nickname because he was a medical doctor, joined the New York Knickerbocker Base Ball Club in 1845. He began work on setting standards for the sport, both in its rules and in its equipment. He himself made hundreds of balls for the Knickerbockers and for other teams that wanted to get organized. In 1856, the 12 baseball teams that existed at the time organized a national convention. They elected Doc president and drafted the "Laws of Base Ball" documents that recently emerged. Those papers sold at auction for $3.26 million in 2016—the third largest purchase of sports memorabilia in history.

Merlin made the unwise decision to combine his interests at a 1760 party in London, England. Wanting to make a grand entrance, he designed a pair of boots equipped with wheels, slipped them on his feet, and rolled into the festivities while playing a violin. It certainly was a spectacle—Merlin hadn't outfitted his skates with a way to turn or brake, so he fiddled his way right into a full-length mirror. Even though Merlin failed spectacularly, roller-skating would go on to become an international craze starting about a century later.

NOBLE
UP-AND-COMERS

◀══ HEIRS TO THE SPORTS THRONE ══▶

Baseball, basketball, and hockey are hailed the kings of American sports today. But they were once no more than oddball activities; it took time for them to rise to the top and earn their spot as sovereigns of all sports. The activities on this page may not wear the crown yet, but just wait—someday, you could be watching some of them in the Olympics.

CHEESE ROLLING

Once a year, people gather on top of Cooper's Hill, near Gloucester, England, to honor the age-old practice of the cheese roll. The game is straightforward enough: Racers line up at the top of the hill, each ready to roll an eight-pound (3.6-kg) wheel of local Double Gloucester cheese down a hill. The first person to the bottom wins the cheese.

If you think this sounds easy, think again. The hill is so steep, racers start in a seated position to keep from falling down the 70-degree slope. Some racing cheese wheels clock in at over 70 miles an hour (112 km/h) on the way down.

People can be, and often are, taken to the hospital for broken bones—competitors and spectators alike. Think what you will about the time-honored event, but make no mistake: The cheese roll is no cakewalk!

UNDERWATER HOCKEY

The objective of underwater hockey is the same as every other variety of the sport, be it ice, field, or floor: Two teams use sticks to push a puck into a goal. The big difference here is that the game is played on the bottom of a swimming pool—with no breathable oxygen surrounding the puck.

Underwater hockey is played in 36 countries on every inhabited continent. World championships are held under its governing international body, the World Underwater Federation, an organization recognized by the International Olympic Committee. Even so, it may be a while before underwater hockey is an Olympic sport—so don't hold your breath.

letting it touch the ground on your side. And like soccer, you can't use your arms or hands.

But this sport—native to Southeast Asia—is no mash-up. The high-flying kicking contest is older than both soccer and volleyball by about 200 years. The sport traces its roots back to Southeast Asia around the 1600s, where it was originally played with balls made from woven dried palm leaves.

QUIDDITCH

Yes, *that* quidditch. The most popular sport of the wizarding realm has come to be embraced by the college-age muggles who grew up with the Harry Potter books. The non-magical version of quidditch is played on the ground by teams of seven players—three chasers, two beaters, a keeper, and a seeker. Only seekers and keepers can use quaffles (volleyballs), and only beaters can touch the bludgers (dodgeballs). And every player must keep mounted on a toy broom at all times.

Everyone, that is, except for the neutral player, who stands in for the most special ball, called the Golden Snitch. Dressed all in yellow, the snitch enters the game in the 18th minute, dashes about unhindered by a broomstick, and does their best to protect the tennis ball stuck to their back.

ZORBING

Another downhill pastime, zorbing was invented in New Zealand in the late 20th century. A zorb is a double-hulled inflatable ball large enough for a grown adult to fit into—in other words, it's a human-size hamster ball. Zorbing courses feature gentle slopes guarded by buffers, walls, and bumpers on either side. These safety measures ensure rolling inside a giant ball stays exactly as fun as it sounds.

SEPAK TAKRAW

If you happened to catch a game of sepak takraw, you might think it's a sport of soccer meets volleyball. The objective is, indeed, very much like volleyball: Knock the ball to the ground on the other side of a net without

GEORGE WILLIAMS

➤ A PLACE TO BELONG ═╍●

The Industrial Revolution that took place in the late 1700s and early 1800s was a time of great change in London, England. Lured by the promise of a steady paycheck, young men from England's rural areas flocked to the city in droves. But the conditions they found there were dire: Factory workers were poor, sick, overworked, and overcrowded. Upon seeing what was becoming of the youth of London, one young man resolved to do something to improve lives of the other young men in the city.

ON THE ROAD TO LONDON

George Williams knew about the problems facing London's youth because he experienced them himself. When he was just 20 years old, he had moved from his birthplace in rural Somerset, England, to the bustling city of London to work in the booming textile industry. He was shocked by what he found there.

Williams got a good job as a sales assistant in a fabric shop. He was able to afford adequate housing, but he saw that in much of the city, several families crammed into a single apartment. Because coal was the fuel of the day, and because the city was so jam-packed with people, the air in London was choked with soot. The river often reeked of sewage, people suffered from a lack of clean water, and wave after wave of disease rocked the city. Worse still, Williams discovered that many of the city's factory workers were children often much younger than 10 years old. They worked up to 12 hours a day, six days a week. Many of them

> Today, the YMCA serves more than 45 million people in 119 countries.

ROYAL RUNDOWN

➤→ **BORN:** October 11, 1821, Somerset, England   ➤→ **DIED:** November 6, 1905, London, England
➤→ **LED:** The YMCA   ➤→ **REMEMBERED FOR:** Founding the world's largest youth charity

For decades, the YMCA has helped keep kids active and healthy through sports programs and other activities.

worked in factories with toxic chemicals or dangerous machines, and they often became sick or injured. What little time young men had between factory work and unsanitary living conditions they spent on London's crime-ridden streets. Even though he was only 22 years old himself, Williams hatched a plan to right some of the wrongs he witnessed.

THE YOUNG MEN'S CHRISTIAN ASSOCIATION

In 1844, Williams gathered together a group of 11 other concerned young men in the store where he worked. Together, they held the first meeting of the Young Men's Christian Association (YMCA). As a devout Christian, Williams was worried over the safety of the young men of London, but he was also worried for their souls. So at first, the Y was mostly a place for Bible study and prayer. But over time, it came to provide young men with lodging and a place to get exercise, too.

By 1851, there were 24 Ys in Great Britain. That same year, the idea spread to Montreal, Canada, and to Boston, Massachusetts, U.S.A. Soon, the organization began popping up all over the world. In the 1880s, YMCAs began constructing their own buildings with gyms, swimming pools, and bowling alleys. Dormitories provided members with a safe, clean place to live. Members led exercise classes, organized humanitarian efforts—and even invented basketball (p. 116)!

Eventually, the YMCA came to be a place for everyone, of any gender, race, religion, or nationality. Williams lived long enough to see his YMCA in 45 locations serving an astounding 700,000 members. For his service, he was knighted by Queen Victoria in 1894.

◄─◆─►

RIGHTING A WRONG
Anthony Bowen (1809–1871)

When the YMCA first opened its doors in the United States, in 1851, young black men were not allowed to join. Two years later, Anthony Bowen righted that wrong when he opened the first YMCA that welcomed African-American boys.

Born a slave in Maryland in 1809, Bowen managed to save up enough money to purchase his freedom: $425. Bowen proceeded to devote his new, free life to serving others, with the YMCA he opened in Washington, D.C. Poet Langston Hughes would attend that Y, as would future Supreme Court Justice Thurgood Marshall and basketball star Elgin Baylor. Those young men and countless other boys and girls in D.C. have the efforts of Anthony Bowen to thank for a safe place to play, grow, and learn.

RULERS OF
THEIR GAME

Sports Superstars

Even in the world of professional sports, where every competitor is an elite performer, there are a few stars who just shine brighter. These athletes are the best of the best, and their skills on the court, field, or track make them fan favorites to boot. Here are some of today's athletes who stand at the top of their game.

KING OF KICKS:
Lionel Messi (1987–)

Today, Lionel Messi is considered the best player of the most popular sport in the world: football (soccer to Americans). But that future once seemed impossible: When he was a kid, Messi was diagnosed with a disorder that prevented him from growing. But he was also a superstar soccer player who was recruited by the Barcelona football club when he was just 13 years old. Part of Messi's contract promised that the football club would pay for medical treatments that helped him reach five feet seven inches (1.7 m). But Messi has reached greater heights than that. He is the only footballer in history who's won the coveted European Golden Shoe award five times, given to the sport's top goal scorer each year. Despite his mountain of other awards and honors, Messi remains humble and generous, funding medical treatments, centers, and research for kids battling illness like he did.

KING OF THE COURT:
LeBron James (1984–)

These days, when most people think of King James, they aren't thinking of England. They're considering the kid from Akron, Ohio, U.S.A., who grew up to become the best basketball player in a generation—some say, in the history of the sport. LeBron James has won four NBA Most Valuable Player awards, three national championships, and two Olympic gold medals. He's been the biggest name in basketball for the better part of two decades. And his success on the court is matched only by his achievements in business. In 2016, James signed a lifetime endorsement deal with Nike worth one billion dollars—the first athlete to do so. When he's not shooting hoops, he's working with kids and parents in need for his LeBron James Family Foundation.

SULTAN OF SPEED:
Usain Bolt (1986–)

When he was growing up in the island nation of Jamaica, Usain Bolt loved playing the sport of cricket. He was especially skilled at racing down the pitch to score. His coaches were so astounded by his speed that they began encouraging him to switch sports and train as a sprinter. It wasn't long before Bolt was living up to his name, shredding records at track-and-field events and collecting nine gold medals over four Olympic Games. He gave his best performance in Berlin, Germany, on August 16, 2008, running the 100-meter dash in 9.572 seconds—making him the fastest man in history! Bolt is as savvy in business as he is fast on the track, securing sponsorships that make him one of the highest-paid athletes in the world. And his Usain Bolt Foundation helps create educational opportunities for kids around the globe.

RULER OF THE RACETRACK:
Richard Petty (1937–)

The first car race was held in 1895, and the winner averaged a poky 15 miles an hour (24 km/h). Things have sped up since then: By the time NASCAR was founded, in 1948, cars had improved tremendously and so had the skills of drivers. And from 1958 to 1992, one driver in particular reigned supreme. Nicknamed "the King," Richard Petty won 200 races, almost twice as many as any other driver! During Richard's time on the track, his racing team made several important innovations that revolutionized the sport, including the addition of roll bars to the cars, helmets that cooled the driver's head, and two-way radios between the driver and the pit crew. Richard Petty became such an icon that the crowd at his final race in 1992 included U.S. president George H. W. Bush.

COMMANDING QUEENS

QUEEN OF THE BEAM
Simone Biles (1997–)

At four feet nine inches (1.4 m), Simone Biles may be small—even for a gymnast—but her performance makes her tower over the competition. Many experts call Biles the best gymnast in the world. She sprints powerfully across the mats and propels herself high into the air as she tumbles across the floor and springs off the vault. And with her confident demeanor, she makes flying through the air look easy. She was already the three-time defending gymnastics world champion before the 2016 Summer Olympics in Rio de Janeiro, Brazil, where she led the U.S. women's team to the gold and dominated the competition herself, scooping up first-place medals in vault, floor, and individual all-around. With 19 Olympic and World Championship medals to her name, Biles is the most decorated American gymnast in history.

ALEX HONNOLD

⟨═══ FREE-SOLOING SUPERSTAR ═══⟩

Rock climbing already seems daring enough. But imagine scaling a sheer wall with not even a rope to keep you from plummeting hundreds of feet if you slip! That's free soloing—a style of climbing in which climbers scramble up rock faces without safety gear of any kind.

The undisputed king of free soloing is Alex Honnold, who earned the nickname "No Big Deal" for uttering the phrase after completing death-defying feats far beyond the reach of most human beings. Though Honnold has completed several impressive free-solo climbs that rocked the climbing world, he's most famous for free soloing El Capitan, a mountain wall in Yosemite National Park that punches more than half a mile (0.8 km) into the sky. It's considered one of the toughest climbs in the sport. Imagine scaling the world's tallest building with just your hands and feet—and you're not even halfway there yet.

On June 3, 2017, Honnold pulled on a pair of grippy climbing shoes, strapped a bag of chalk around his waist for keeping his hands dry, and found his first toehold at the base of El Capitan. In just under four hours, Honnold pulled his body over the rocky lip at the peak and stood on top of the mountain he had conquered. Many say it's the greatest achievement in the history of the sport, and it's documented in the 2018 film *Free Solo*.

Honnold practiced for the event obsessively, doing one-armed push-ups and hanging by his fingertips for an hour every other day. But many think it's Honnold's mental ability that makes him truly great. Neuroscientists have even studied his brain to see how it responds to fear. They found that Honnold has trained himself to remain calm in the scariest situations—like dangling 3,000 feet (914 m) above oblivion with nothing to stop his fall. Talk about a head for heights!

> "For me the crucial question is not how to climb without fear—that's impossible—but how to deal with it when it creeps into your nerve endings."
> —Alex Honnold

ROYAL RUNDOWN

➤ **BORN:** August 17, 1985, Sacramento, California, U.S.A. ➤ **LEADS:** Free-solo rock climbing ➤ **KNOWN FOR:** Free soloing El Capitan

JIMMY CHIN

⊶═ ADVENTURE PHOTOGRAPHER ═➤

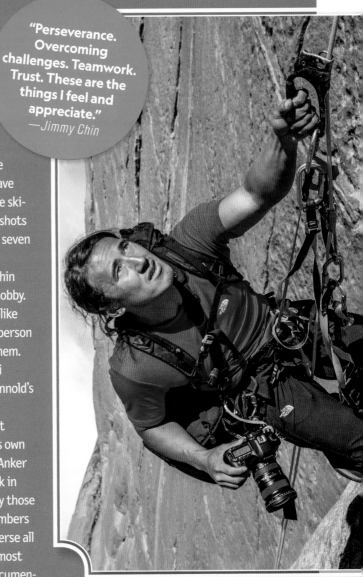

Here's something to consider: All the pictures of Alex Honnold as he made history pulling himself up El Capitan without a safety net were taken by someone making *the exact same climb*—only that person also had to carry a camera (though he did use safety ropes!).

That climber with the camera was Jimmy Chin, an athlete of exceptional skill with an eye for important moments. His photos, which have been published everywhere from *National Geographic* to the *New York Times Magazine*, have inspired a whole new generation of mountain climbers, alpine skiers, and other outdoor thrill-seekers. Chin's library includes shots from the tops of the highest mountain peaks on each of the seven continents—including Mount Everest.

Known for his talent at capturing immense landscapes, Chin originally started snapping to fund his mountain-climbing hobby. He considers it a personal challenge to take photographs unlike anything ever seen before. His photographs often include a person dwarfed by the vastness of the natural world surrounding them.

Chin is also a high-flying filmmaker: He and Elizabeth Chai Vasarhelyi, his wife and filmmaking partner, documented Honnold's efforts to make climbing history on El Capitan in National Geographic's 2018 film *Free Solo*. And Chin has also gotten out from behind the camera in a documentary he shot about his own attempt to tackle Mount Meru with fellow climbers Conrad Anker and Renan Ozturk. Meru, a nearly 22,000-foot (6,705-m) peak in northern India's Himalayan mountain range, is considered by those in the climbing world to be tougher than Mount Everest. Climbers have to carry 200 pounds (91 kg) of gear and be able to traverse all kinds of terrain, including a 1,500-foot (457-m) stretch of almost totally smooth granite. Chin's taking the world of nature documentary to new heights: *Free Solo* won the 2019 Oscar for Best Documentary Feature.

> "Perseverance. Overcoming challenges. Teamwork. Trust. These are the things I feel and appreciate."
> —Jimmy Chin

ROYAL RUNDOWN

➤➤ **BORN:** October 12, 1973, Mankato, Minnesota, U.S.A. ➤➤ **LEADS:** The highest peak on every continent ➤➤ **KNOWN FOR:** Documenting death-defying climbs

RULER OF
THE RING

Once in a generation there comes an athlete who not only dominates in his sport but also reshapes the culture of his country. Champion boxer Muhammad Ali was that kind of sports superstar. Born Cassius Clay on January 17, 1942, in Louisville, Kentucky, U.S.A., Ali took a new name and became invincible in the ring for the first 11 years of his career. But Ali also took on other battles—working tirelessly for equality and peace. Throughout his life, he fought against the social injustice that he and other black people faced and traveled the world to bring attention to the plight of children and others victimized by conflict. In 1998, Ali was named a United Nations Messenger of Peace. Read on to learn more about the king of the ring.

GAME-CHANGING GLOVES

Boxing gloves have come a long way since they were invented in 1743, when they were typically lined with wool or horsehair. The gloves Ali wore, made by a company founded in 1910, included foam padding and laces for a secure fit. These exact gloves sold for $956,000 at an auction in 2015.

TWO FOR TWO

A year before this famous May 25, 1965, photo was taken, Sonny Liston, the man on the ground, had lost the title of Heavyweight Champion of the World to Muhammad Ali. It was one of the biggest upsets in the history of boxing, and Liston was determined to show the world that Ali's victory had been a fluke. So Liston challenged Ali to a rematch. But the 22-year-old Ali defeated Liston a second time, forcing the boxing world to acknowledge him as the true reigning champion.

From Gold Medal ...

America first met Muhammad Ali when he won gold in the 1960 Olympic Games in Rome. Ali was severely disappointed that even after winning a gold medal for his country, many of his countrymen still treated him like a second-class citizen because of the color of his skin. There were restaurants in his hometown of Louisville, Kentucky, that still wouldn't serve him even though he was an American Olympian.

... To Freedom Medal

Two years after this knock-out photo (left) was taken, Muhammad Ali made waves in America by refusing to fight in the Vietnam War, declaring himself a conscientious objector. He was arrested and found guilty by a jury for refusing to serve, but Ali stood up for his beliefs. Many criticized Ali's decision: He was stripped of the title he won for defeating Sonny Liston and even had his boxing license taken away in 1966. Thirty-four years later, after the tireless work of Ali and many others like him, President George W. Bush recognized Ali with the Presidential Medal of Freedom.

QUICK WORK

In professional boxing, a bout ends if one athlete is knocked out, or KO'd. If neither boxer is KO'd, it ends at the end of the 15th round. Liston was fiercely determined to reclaim his title, and many expected the fight to be a nail biter. But Ali stunned the crowd by knocking Liston out near the end of only the first round. Spectators were stunned, and many hadn't even seen Ali connecting with Liston. The moment became famously known as the "Phantom Punch."

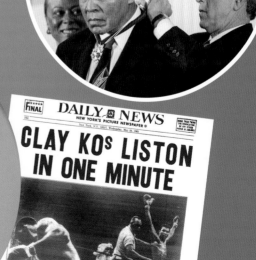

FINAL · **DAILY NEWS** · NEW YORK'S PICTURE NEWSPAPER

CLAY KOs LISTON IN ONE MINUTE

KINGS OF CHANGE

Many of history's kings have focused only on the tasks right in front of them: winning the battle, feeding the people, keeping the throne. But it's also the job of a truly great leader to look beyond the next step and peer into the future instead. From conservationists working to preserve the planet for the next generation to computer scientists finding ways to create intelligent machines, these big thinkers are hard at work planning for the future. Get ready to meet a group of innovators and earthshakers who kept their eye on the world of tomorrow.

Steve Jobs, holding an iPad at a conference in San Francisco, California, U.S.A., in 2010

JADAV PAYENG

⟤ THE FOREST MAN OF INDIA ⟥

> **"Cut me before you cut my trees!"**
> —Jadav Payeng

Every day for nearly four decades, Jadav Payeng has risen before dawn. He bicycles an hour to the shore, then boards a small boat and rows a short distance from the mainland of India to a small island in the middle of a river. Then he begins his daily work: bringing the once bare landscape back to life.

LIFE ON THE EDGE

Payeng is from the state of Assam, in northeast India, which is dominated by the mighty Brahmaputra River. Every year when the monsoon season comes, the floodwaters turn the river into a giant blade that carves larger and larger segments of sandy soil from the riverbank. In the middle of this river sits the largest river island in the world, Majuli. More than 160,000 people live here, and during flooding season, their homes become danger zones. Every year, homes are destroyed and huge areas of land are eroded away. Over the past 100 years, 70 percent of Majuli has disappeared. What's left has become a wasteland.

In 1979, Payeng came across a mudflat where dozens and dozens of snakes were washed up. Unable to find shade, the animals had died from exposure to the extreme heat of the mudflats. Payeng was shocked by the sight. It made him realize that if the people of Majuli didn't do something, they were going to suffer the same fate as the snakes.

FROM SEED TO FOREST

Payeng knew that trees help prevent erosion by holding soil in place and sheltering it from wind and rain. So the young man appealed to local officials to immediately start planting trees on Majuli. But the officials had their own flood-control plans in mind: to build large concrete floodgates to try to tame

ROYAL RUNDOWN

➤ **BORN:** 1959 ➤ **LEADS:** The Molai Forest ➤ **KNOWN FOR:**
A hand-planted forest bigger than New York City's Central Park

Payeng transformed a barren desert into an extensive forest.

the river. Payeng didn't want to rely on them to save Majuli, so he decided to take matters into his own hands.

Payeng began planting trees in the bare earth: first bamboo, then cotton. Slowly, his saplings took hold, rooted, and stretched new leaves skyward. Grasses from upriver washed into the new foliage and sprouted, too. All the while, Payeng tended to his wild garden. Now in his mid-50s, he's been planting every day since he was 16. For his lifetime spent reviving the earth, he's earned a nickname: the Forest Man of India.

STILL GROWING

Where there once was a barren desert, there is now a thriving ecosystem brought back from the brink. It even has a name: the Molai Forest, and it stretches over nearly 1,400 acres (567 ha). In satellite photos, the forest is an emerald haven surrounded by lifeless silt. It's hard to believe it was hand-planted by one person. After decades of difficult labor, the vibrant forest has compelled wildlife to move back to the once desolate part of Majuli island; it is now populated by tigers, rhinos, deer, and elephants.

People only began to take notice of Payeng's project around 2008. But since then, he has been honored all across India and has earned the respect and gratitude of people all over the world. Today, Payeng welcomes visitors from every corner of the map, who come to see his island forest. All he asks before they leave is that they plant a tree.

HER DEEPNESS
Sylvia Earle
(1935–)

Saving the planet doesn't only mean protecting the land. Nicknamed "Her Deepness," Sylvia Earle has been the queen of ocean exploration and conservation for more than 40 years. Since her first dive at age 16, she has spent more than 7,000 hours—nearly a year in total!—underwater. In 1970, she led a group of five women scientists who lived in a capsule 1,250 feet (381 m) below the surface for a record-setting two weeks straight. Earle has conducted groundbreaking research on algae, tracked marine mammals as they crossed oceans, and discovered many new species of aquatic life. She was the first woman to be appointed chief scientist of the National Oceanic and Atmospheric Administration, and she was National Geographic's first female explorer-in-residence. Today, Earle devotes her time to raising awareness about the dire problems the ocean faces: floating patches of garbage the size of small countries, coral reefs that are rapidly disappearing, and overfishing that has reduced the populations of large fish like halibut and sharks to less than 10 percent of what they were 70 years ago.

NOBLE **NOBELS**

Changing the World for the Better

Every year since 1901, the Nobel Peace Prize has been awarded to one person who is working to make the world better, safer, and happier. These five were honored with the Nobel Prize for their work improving lives, raising hope, and standing up to hatred and bigotry.

PEACEFUL PROTESTER:
Liu Xiaobo (1955–2017)

While China's economy has grown tremendously in the 21st century, many would say that its government's attitude toward human rights has fallen far behind. Liu Xiaobo was one of the brave Chinese citizens who dared to speak out against the ruling Communist Party. He first rose into the public eye during the 1989 Tiananmen Square demonstrations, when the Chinese government met peaceful protesters with brutal violence. Xiaobo saved lives by persuading some protesters to leave rather than face down government tanks. He advocated for reform in China's government, contributing to documents like "Charter 08," which called for a new government with a constitution and a representative democracy. In 2009, Xiaobo was arrested by Chinese authorities and sentenced to 11 years in prison. The following year, he was awarded the Nobel Peace Prize for his nonviolent resistance against the Chinese government.

DARING DIPLOMAT:
Kofi Annan (1938–2018)

Few people did as much for the global community as Kofi Annan, a two-term secretary-general of the United Nations. Annan, who was born in Ghana, studied science, economics, and international affairs. He combined all of his passions when he began working for the World Health Organization in 1962; he later went on to specialize in providing health care for refugees displaced by war. Annan led 70,000 United Nations civilian and military peacekeepers in the mid-1990s before becoming the UN's chief officer: the secretary-general. In that role, Annan oversaw dozens of peace projects all over the world, from Iraq to East Timor. On the side, he found time to help the UN raise $1.5 billion for a global AIDS and health fund. Annan was honored with the Nobel Peace Prize in 2001.

VOICE OF THE VOICELESS:
Elie Wiesel (1928–2016)

Romanian-born Elie Wiesel was only a teenager when he and his family were deported to Auschwitz concentration camp in Poland in 1944. There, his mother and younger sister perished, and young Elie and his father were forced into hard labor. As Allied forces advanced ever closer, they and thousands of other prisoners were marched to Buchenwald concentration camp in Germany. It was there that Wiesel's father died—and from there that Wiesel was liberated by Allied forces in April 1945.

After the war, Wiesel went to Paris, where he attended school and worked as a journalist. He arrived in the United States in 1956, and he became a professor and an author. Over the following decades, through books, interviews, and lectures, Wiesel recounted his experiences as a survivor of the Holocaust and drew the world's attention to its horrors. He spoke out on behalf of persecuted people and against hatred, oppression, and violence. For his advocacy and his contributions, he was awarded the Nobel Peace Prize in 1986 and the Presidential Medal of Freedom in 1992.

PRESIDENTIAL PEACEMAKER:
Jimmy Carter (1924–)

As the 39th president of the United States, Jimmy Carter led the nation from 1977 to 1981, a time of serious strife. America was reeling from the aftereffects of a political scandal that had occurred under the previous president and was also struggling with racial tensions, high oil prices, and tough relations with the Middle East. Many American voters thought Carter mishandled these issues, and he was not reelected for a second term. But it was during his time as president that he began a focus on the diplomacy that would later win him the Nobel Prize. Vowing to make worldwide human rights a priority, Carter suspended aid to countries such as Nicaragua and Chile, where human rights violations were taking place. And most famously, with his Camp David Accords, Carter acted as a mediator between longtime enemies Egypt and Israel, helping broker a landmark peace treaty. Once out of office, Carter threw himself into his mission to wage peace. Through his organization the Carter Center, he has worked globally to promote human rights, fight preventable diseases, and help ensure fair elections in developing countries. He was awarded the Nobel Peace Prize in 2002.

COMMANDING QUEENS

CIVILIAN PROTECTOR
Jody Williams (1950–)

Though the Nobel Peace Prize has been awarded for more than a century, only 16 women have ever won. One of them is Jody Williams, who received the award in 1997 for her efforts to eradicate land mines. These explosive devices are planted in times of war, and today, millions of them lurk beneath the countryside in war-torn areas. Many are detonated by innocent civilians. Every year at least 15,000 people are either killed or maimed for life by leftover land mines. Williams, as the chief strategist of the International Campaign to Ban Landmines, has gotten 120 countries to promise not to use the devices, to spare future civilian suffering. Many countries have gone so far as to destroy their stockpile of land mines so that they can never be used again. Beginning in 2006, Williams expanded her efforts to build peace by co-founding the Nobel Women's Initiative, an organization that brings together the living female Nobel laureates to use their influence to support women around the world working toward peace, justice, and equality.

CONFUCIUS

⫸—= THE GREAT SAGE =—⊶

"They must often change who would be constant in happiness or wisdom."
—Confucius

Confucius was arguably the single most influential figure in Chinese history. Aspects of his teachings would come to shape the spiritual and cultural lives of China, Korea, Japan, and other East Asian countries for thousands of years.

He was born around 551 B.C., a turbulent time in his homeland. Some two centuries before his birth, the Zhou dynasty's effort to unify the country had come undone. When the fractured Chinese states weren't fighting with each other, they were at their northern borders trying to stave off Mongol raiding parties. That fighting broke down into civil war, as China's territories turned against each other during the Warring States Period, from 475 to 221 B.C.

It is from this chaos that Confucius would emerge. Some accounts say he was born to a royal family; others say he was a commoner. But no matter his origins, Confucius developed a passion for learning from a young age. He came to believe that through thinking and learning, people could transform their lives and change society for the better. He mastered everything from poetry and history to calligraphy and even archery. Then he traveled away from his home in the state of Lu, preaching his ideas as he went.

Confucius's philosophy was based on the Golden Rule: treating others as you would wish to be treated. He encouraged people to lead moral lives, respect their elders, and pay homage to their ancestors. Most importantly for the future of China, Confucius preached the importance of levelheaded leaders. He called on kings and princes to be humble and lead by example, motivating their subjects to lead good lives by leading good lives themselves. His teachings have outlasted him by thousands of years: Confucianism is still widely practiced today.

ROYAL RUNDOWN

➤ **BORN:** ca September 28, 551 B.C., Lu, ancient China   ➤ **DIED:** 479 B.C., Lu, ancient China
➤ **LED:** Chinese philosophy   ➤ **REMEMBERED FOR:** Confucianism, a belief system followed for more than two millennia

SOCRATES

WISEST AMONG THE GREEKS

For centuries, ancient Greeks would travel high up the slope of Mount Parnassus to consult the mystical oracle at Delphi. It was believed that the oracle could speak the wisdom of the gods to ordinary people. So it was a big endorsement when, according to ancient Greek legend, the oracle proclaimed Socrates the wisest person in Greece.

Before he devoted himself to thinking about life's big questions, Socrates had been a soldier. He served the Greek city-state of Athens during its Golden Age and once rescued a future statesman and general of Athens, named Alcibiades, during a siege in 432 B.C. After his days in the military, Socrates began his contemplations on philosophy—and it was then that he learned about what the oracle had said.

Socrates refused to believe it. He didn't think that he was wisest of the Greeks, so he set out to investigate the words of the oracle by questioning people he knew to be wiser than he. Slowly, Socrates came to realize that men he once considered wise were often pretending to know more than they did. And his tactic of questioning began what would come to be called the Socratic method, a way of learning through critical thinking.

The Socratic method gave people a new way to think, but it ultimately ended Socrates' life. His constant questioning of everything meant he spent a lot of time challenging authority. In 399 B.C., he was arrested and charged with corrupting the students of Athens by encouraging them to think for themselves instead of accepting the rules of society. He was condemned to death, but his lessons survived by passing to his student Plato, then on to Plato's student Aristotle, and from Aristotle to the foundations of Western civilization.

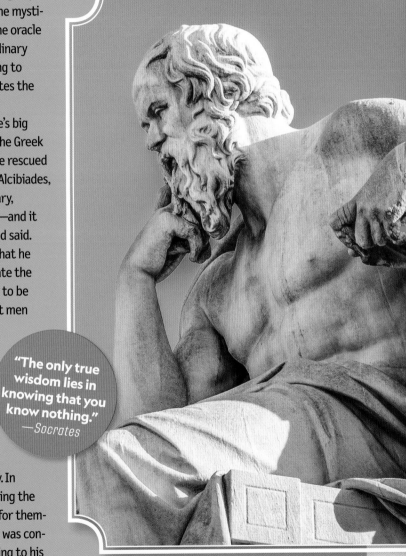

"The only true wisdom lies in knowing that you know nothing."
—*Socrates*

ROYAL RUNDOWN

➡➤ **BORN:** ca 470 B.C., Alopece, ancient Greece ➡➤ **DIED:** 399 B.C., classical Athens
➡➤ **LED:** Greek philosophy ➡➤ **REMEMBERED FOR:** The Socratic method of learning

CELEBRITIES WORTH **CELEBRATING**

Using Fame for Good

Being a celebrity might sound like it's all one big party: big house, fancy car, and lots of attention. But to some celebrities, that public position carries with it a responsibility to do good in the world. These people have used their star power to make the future a brighter place—and that makes them real Hollywood royalty.

FUNDING THE FUTURE:
Will Smith (1968–)

This versatile rapper turned actor made his first million before he could legally vote. Will Smith came to fame along with his friend DJ Jazzy Jeff with their 1987 debut album, *Rock the House.* From there, Smith took his popular persona to television in the long-running and well-loved '90s sitcom *The Fresh Prince of Bel-Air.* In the mid-1990s, Smith jumped from TV star to bona fide movie star, appearing in blockbusters such as *Independence Day, Men in Black,* and *Wild Wild West.*

But Smith isn't just one of the most popular actors of his day—he's also one of the most generous. Along with his wife, Jada Pinkett Smith, he has given away millions of dollars to causes as varied as his career. Education has long been near the top of the couple's list; they have supported historically black colleges, the American Film Institute, and the undergraduate film program at New York University. In 2012, they visited Ethiopia to help raise money to provide water for developing nations. And in 2017, they even auctioned off clothing from their personal collections to raise money for disaster relief in the Caribbean.

SELFLESS STUNTMAN:
Jackie Chan (1954–)

He's an actor, a martial artist, a director, a producer, and a singer, but Jackie Chan is most famous for performing his own stunts. He holds the Guinness World Record for most stunts performed by a living actor. But it was a stunt gone wrong that changed his life—and the lives of countless others—for the better.

HUMANITARIAN HEAVYWEIGHT:
John Cena (1977–)

Many celebrities donate money, but there is perhaps no one who gives more of his time than wrestler and actor John Cena. He is incredibly successful in the ring, having won 25 championships and 16 world champion titles. He calls his wrestling persona a "goody-two-shoes Superman," but his real-life personality isn't far off: He has used his popularity to champion anti-bullying campaigns, support the pro-LGBTQ rights NOH8 Campaign, and help raise more than two million dollars to fight breast cancer.

Cena is especially popular with kids. "Meeting John Cena" has topped the list of wishes at the Make-A-Wish Foundation for years now, and Cena has made that wish come true more than 500 times; that's nearly a year and half worth of days spent with kids who need it the most. What's more, he's donated more than six million of his own airline miles for wishers who needed to travel. Forget wrestling records: This star holds the Make-A-Wish record for most wishes granted.

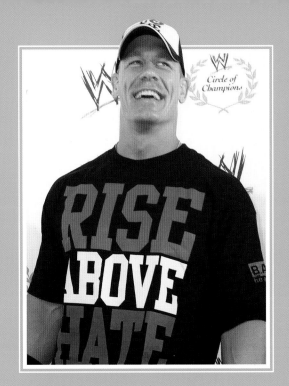

STAR BENEFACTOR:
Paul Newman (1935–2008)

He was one of the most celebrated movie stars of the 20th century, but Paul Newman came close to ending his career with his very first movie. Called *The Silver Chalice* (1954), it was so bad that Newman himself took out a full-page ad in a trade newspaper apologizing for it! Luckily, Hollywood realized Newman's true talent. He eventually made his mark in classics such as *Cool Hand Luke* (1967), *Butch Cassidy and the Sundance Kid* (1969), and *The Sting* (1973).

Newman's journey to philanthropy got an unusual start. During Christmas of 1980, he decided to mix up some homemade salad dressing in his barn to give away to his neighbors. One of them was food and lifestyle superstar Martha Stewart, who entered the dressing in a taste test—and it won. Newman started selling the dressing in 1982, and by the end of the year, he had made the choice to donate all the profits to charity. In the years since, Newman's Own grew to develop a range of products, including popcorn, frozen pizza, and salsa. To date, the Newman's Own Foundation has given away more than $500 million.

Chan was filming an action movie in 1986 when he missed a jump and landed on his head. Before then, he hadn't been very involved in charity work, sometimes turning down requests because he was so busy. But as the actor was rushed to the hospital, he promised himself that if he survived, he would dedicate his life to helping others. He kept his word. Chan founded the Dragon's Heart Foundation to build schools in needy areas of China. Beginning in 2006, the martial arts master has matched every dollar donated to the cause.

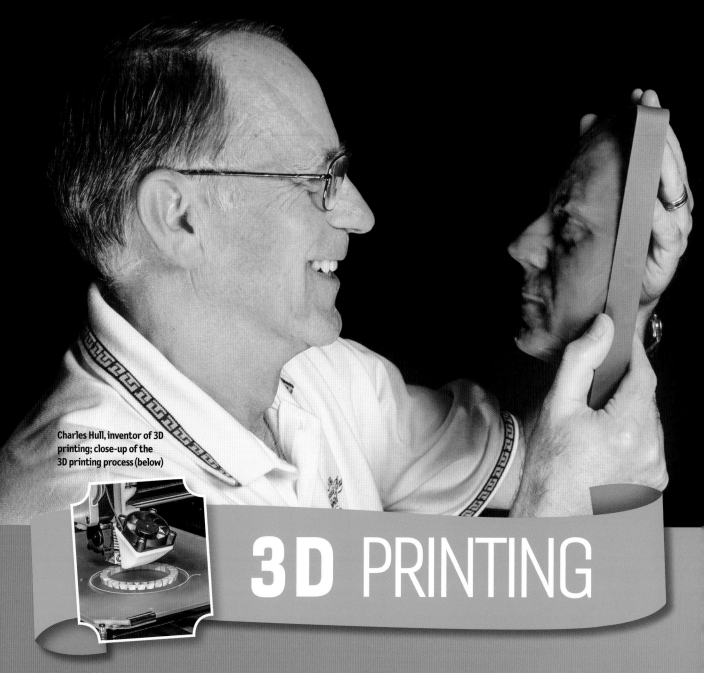

Charles Hull, inventor of 3D
printing; close-up of the
3D printing process (below)

3D PRINTING

NOBLE TECHNOLOGY OF TOMORROW

Originally developed by inventor Charles Hull in 1986, 3D printing is among the most earth-shaking technologies of the early 21st century. Most 3D printers work by taking a computer model of an object and turning it into lots of thin cross-sections—like slicing a loaf of bread. The computer then tells a small robotic arm how to move as it squeezes out fast-cooling plastic goop in the shape of those slices. Laying down layer by layer, the printer turns the model into a real-life object. Today, 3D printers can be purchased for a few hundred dollars—opening the door for intrepid inventors to create blueprints for all kinds of amazing 3D-printed devices. Here are a few of their most stand-out inventions.

INSTRUMENTS

In 2014, a student band in Lund, Sweden, got together to put on a show. That wasn't so unusual—except that every instrument they were playing was 3D printed, and it was the first performance of its kind. Developed by a professor at Lund University, the band included a drum, a keyboard, and two guitars. Though 3D-printing instruments is an expensive process for now, it could someday provide access to musical instruments to people all over the world.

PROSTHETIC LIMBS

Traditional prosthetic limbs can be expensive—some cost as much as $50,000—and last for only a few years before

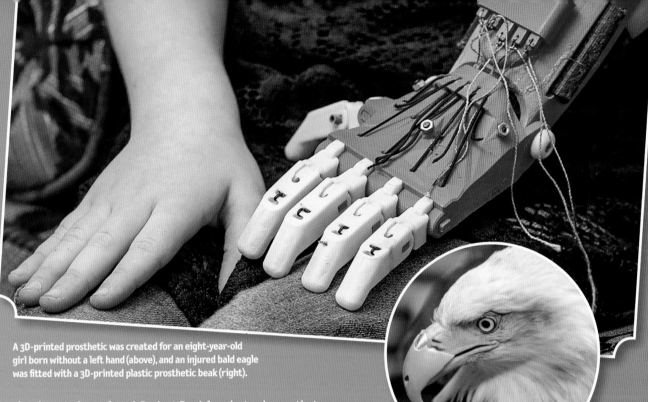

A 3D-printed prosthetic was created for an eight-year-old girl born without a left hand (above), and an injured bald eagle was fitted with a 3D-printed plastic prosthetic beak (right).

they have to be replaced. Project Daniel seeks to change that by providing victims of war-torn Sudan with affordable plastic limbs. For now, the printed arms can't compete with top-of-the-line models in terms of strength and finger control. But at a price of around $100 each, they make prosthetic limbs accessible for people who otherwise would have to go without them.

HOUSES

As more and more people inhabit planet Earth, we're faced with an increasing problem: Where are they all going to live? One company in San Francisco, California, U.S.A., is hoping to make the affordable houses of the future using a supersize version of a 3D printer. Instead of plastic, it prints with concrete, and instead of costing hundreds of thousands of dollars and taking months to build, its houses cost just over $10,000 and print in less than 24 hours. The technology is still in development, but in the future, it could revolutionize the way people find a home.

A WRENCH

When we're already printing everything from houses to hands, what's the big deal about a 3D-printed wrench? The ratchet wrench in question is special because it wasn't made on Earth; it was made 254 miles (409 km) above it! The test wrench was printed in 2016 on board the International Space Station and was an important first step toward establishing a way to manufacture parts and tools in orbit. Sending material into space is extremely expensive, costing about $10,000 for every pound. The ability to instead 3D-print objects as they are needed would save space missions millions of dollars. Astronauts could use the technology to build not only replacements for broken parts but one day even entire spaceships.

The world's first totally 3D-printed house, in Tongzhou District, Beijing, China (center). Comedian Jay Leno holds a wrench he created with a 3D printer in his garage in Burbank, California, U.S.A. (bottom).

LOUIS BRAILLE

⟩━ A TRUE VISIONARY ━╾━•

In 1808, Napoleon's armies were storming across Europe. Though the army was extremely successful, French officers were often frustrated by soldiers who would foolishly light candles or lanterns to read incoming orders at night—giving away their position to the enemy. Napoleon demanded a solution to the problem, and one of his officers, a man named Charles Barbier, developed a system called "night writing" that used raised dots to represent letters or sounds. It was a precursor to the braille system still in use today.

A LIFE-CHANGING ACCIDENT

One year after this event, Louis Braille was born to a family in a small town just east of Paris, France. When he was three years old, he was playing in the shop of his father, a leatherworker, when a sharp tool hit him in the eye. The injury became infected, spread to both eyes, and young Braille was struck blind. His mother was determined that her son would get an education despite his disability, so Braille spent the next seven years hard at work in school.

When he was 10, Braille won a scholarship to the Royal Institute for Blind Youth (now the National Institute for Blind Youth) in Paris. There, he learned to read books made especially for blind people. The letters in these books were raised so they could be felt with the fingertips. But it was extremely difficult to tell one letter apart from another, making the process of reading laborious and slow.

> "In our way, we, the blind, are as indebted to Louis Braille as mankind is to Gutenberg."
> —Helen Keller

SEEING FURTHER

When Louis was 12, a visitor came to the institute. His name was Charles Barbier, and he had created the system that had allowed Napoleon's soldiers to read in complete darkness. The military no

ROYAL RUNDOWN

➤ **BORN:** January 4, 1809, Coupvray, France   ➤ **DIED:** January 6, 1852, Paris, France
➤ **LED:** Education for blind people   ➤ **REMEMBERED FOR:** A refined written language for blind people

Writing letters in Braille (above); a museum in St. Petersburg, Russia, offers a guide specifically for people with visual disabilities (left).

longer used the code, so Barbier had come to the institute to see if it would be of use to the blind children of Paris. Barbier's system of 12 raised bumps arranged in sets of patterns, each representing a different sound, was a huge improvement over raised-word books—but the 12-year-old Braille thought that Barbier's system could be made even better.

For the next three years, Braille spent all of his spare time tinkering with the Barbier system. By the time he was just 15 years old, he had reinvented and refined Barbier's code. The new system was based on six dots instead of 12—meaning each set of dots was small enough that a fingertip could feel them all at once. That made it much easier and faster to read. The new system came to be called braille, and it is still used today all around the world in almost its original form.

LASTING IMPACT

Four years later, Louis Braille became an instructor at the Royal Institute for Blind Youth, the same school he had once attended. He began teaching his system—but was met with resistance by people who did not want to move away from the raised letters they'd been using for 40 years. Braille didn't give up, and by the time he retired in 1850, his new method was gaining support. It spread all over the globe and has since helped millions of people without eyesight live, learn, and lead successful careers.

SYMBOL OF STRENGTH
COMMANDING QUEENS

Helen Keller (1880–1968)

When she was a toddler, Helen Keller was struck with an unknown illness that left her deaf and blind. Curious and intelligent, Keller tried to understand the world around her through touch, smell, and taste. But when she realized that everyone else was communicating with speech—and that she couldn't participate—she became angry. Her family lived in fear of the temper tantrums she threw out of frustration. Many relatives believed Keller should be put in an institution. But everything changed when Keller's parents found her a teacher named Anne Sullivan. With Sullivan's extraordinary guidance, Keller learned to use sign language, read braille, and even speak. She graduated with honors from Radcliffe College in 1904, becoming the first deaf-blind person to earn a bachelor's degree. She went on to write books and lecture on behalf of people living with disabilities, traveling to 35 countries between 1946 and 1957. She campaigned to end malnutrition-caused blindness and established support centers for blind people in the United States. In 1920, she helped found the American Civil Liberties Union, or ACLU.

KINGS OF
TOMORROW

Founding Futurists

The kings of yesteryear knew that the decisions they made could change the world in unpredictable ways. One action could create a series of events that led to either success or chaos. So they turned to oracles, wizards, and sages—people thought to have the power to predict future events. Today's leaders don't need magic. They have futurists: men and women who look ahead and hope to ready us for the world of tomorrow—today!

FORECASTING THE FUTURE:
Raymond Kurzweil (1948–)

At age 17, Ray Kurzweil built a computer that composed piano music. That might not seem like groundbreaking technology now, but in 1965 Kurzweil had a bold vision for the future, one in which humans wouldn't have to teach computers how to do things like compose music—instead, computers would teach themselves! Kurzweil believes that, someday, computers will surpass human levels of intelligence, and he believes it will happen soon—by the year 2029. That prediction might sound crazy, but clearly computers are getting more powerful every day. In fact, Kurzweil went on to develop text-to-speech software for blind people and optical character recognition software, which allows written words to be recognized by a computer. Kurzweil has been making predictions about future events for decades, and many of them have come true, such as that a computer would beat a world chess champion by 1998 (it happened in 1997). Is Kurzweil right about this one, too?

LIVING 1,000 YEARS: Aubrey de Grey (1963–)

Billions of dollars have been raised to fund research aimed at ending ailments like heart disease, cancer, and diabetes. But one man wants to fight more than just disease; he wants to fight death itself. Aubrey de Grey is a biomedical gerontologist (scientist who studies aging) who believes that aging is just another disease—and that it's curable. Scientists at his organization, SENS, are looking for changes in our bodies that cause aging, like the breakdown of our DNA, in the hopes of finding a way of reversing these processes. His research has drawn criticism from the scientific community and from the public, who have voiced fears that his work comes close to tampering with the fundamental laws of nature. But the outcry hasn't stopped de Grey from continuing his research.

COMPUTERS FOR ALL:
Raj Reddy (1937–)

There are two billion people on planet Earth making less than $2.50 a day. Computer scientist Raj Reddy wants to make sure that these people have the same opportunities as everyone else in the modern world. Through his study of human-computer interaction, Reddy has observed that many of the planet's poorest people cannot use computers because they haven't received the reading education necessary to navigate the systems. That's where he comes in. Reddy, a pioneer in the field of speech recognition and winner of the prestigious Turing Award for his work in artificial intelligence, is now working on voice computing. This is a method of interacting with computers that doesn't require the ability to use keyboards or read the labels on desktop icons. Reddy, who was himself born in a small village in southeastern India, hopes to bring the power of technology to all corners of the world.

SIMULATING THE EARTH:
Dirk Helbing (1965–)

In many video games, the player is in charge of a simulated person, town, or theme park. Now imagine a game that puts the player in charge of the entire *world*—that's a little what the Living Earth Simulator is like. The project is led by physicist, mathematician, and sociologist Dirk Helbing at the Swiss Federal Institute of Technology in Zurich, Switzerland. It compiles huge amounts of data: everything from stock prices to government statistics to people's social media posts. Then computer models weave all this information together to make predictions about what will happen in the future. With enough data, Helbing hopes that the Living Earth Simulator will be able to predict everything from wars to disease outbreaks in the hope that Earth's leaders can step in and figure out how to avert these crises before they start. It's an incredibly ambitious project, but it's got backers who believe in it: The Swiss Federal Institute of Technology has invested $1.4 billion into the project.

COMMANDING QUEENS

RULER OF ROBOTICS
Ayanna Howard (1972–)

When Ayanna Howard was a little girl, her favorite TV show was *The Bionic Woman,* which was about a woman who is critically injured by an accident but then gains superhuman powers when she is outfitted with artificial limbs. Fascinated with the idea of using robotics to help people, Howard earned her Ph.D. in electrical engineering, and at age 27, she got her dream job as part of NASA's Jet Propulsion Laboratory in Pasadena, California, U.S.A. There, she led a team of engineers and scientists who worked to develop robots for exploring all kinds of extreme environments—from icy glaciers on Earth to the dusty surface of Mars. She's also the co-founder of Zyrobotics, where part of her work includes developing robotics for kids with disabilities. As a nod to her favorite childhood show, NASA has called Howard their own "bionic woman."

CHRISTIAAN BARNARD

TRAILBLAZER OF HEART TRANSPLANTS

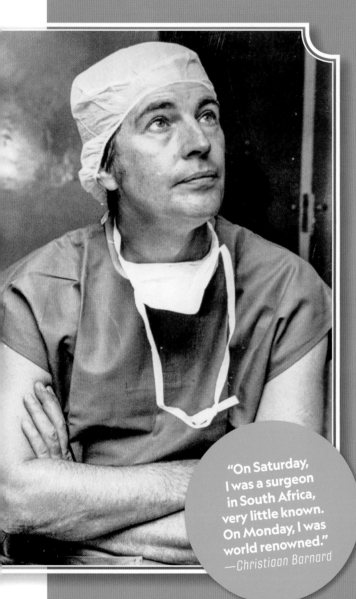

"On Saturday, I was a surgeon in South Africa, very little known. On Monday, I was world renowned."
—Christiaan Barnard

Born in Beaufort West, South Africa, Christiaan Barnard grew up to become one of the most important pioneers in modern medicine. His early interest in the treatment of the brain disease tuberculosis meningitis could have led to a career as a neurosurgeon, but a new wave of excitement over recent successes in open-heart surgery caught Barnard's attention. In 1955, he moved to Minnesota, U.S.A., to train as a heart surgeon.

Barnard was a passionate surgeon, but he had a reputation for being quick-tempered: He was known to become confrontational with nurses and other doctors—even while performing surgery. Sharp tongue aside, Barnard was determined to improve health care. He brought what he had learned back with him to South Africa and quickly put together several high-caliber cardiology surgery departments on his home continent.

In 1967, Barnard teamed up with his brother, Marius, who was also a heart surgeon. Barnard believed he had learned enough about the human heart to try something new— something big. That year, Dr. Christiaan Barnard removed the heart from a man who had just died and placed it in the chest of another man in desperate need of a new heart. This was the world's first heart transplant. Although the person who received the heart lived only 18 more days, the procedure was groundbreaking, and it captured the world's attention.

Barnard continued to improve his technique while others worked to improve anti-rejection drugs, which help prevent a patient's immune system from attacking, or rejecting, the new organ. Since that fateful day in 1967, more than 100,000 heart transplants have been completed by doctors all over the world—life-saving procedures thought impossible until Dr. Barnard learned to trust his instincts and follow his heart.

ROYAL RUNDOWN

➤ **BORN:** November 8, 1922, Beaufort West, South Africa ➤ **DIED:** September 2, 2001, Paphos, Cyprus ➤ **LED:** Cardiothoracic surgery ➤ **REMEMBERED FOR:** The world's first heart transplant

DANIEL HALE WILLIAMS

⊶⊨ PIONEER OF OPEN HEART SURGERY ⊨⇒

When Daniel Hale Williams became a doctor, he was one of only four black physicians in Chicago, Illinois, U.S.A. Wanting to ensure more opportunities for African Americans in medicine, Williams founded the Provident Hospital and Training School for nurses in 1891. It was the first African-American-owned-and-operated hospital in America. There, he helped train a generation of black nurses, physicians, and surgeons. Outside of his role as an educator, Dr. Williams helped to make surgery safer by improving sanitation and sterilization standards in operating rooms across Chicago.

Williams is best remembered for the events that unfolded one night in the summer of 1893. A young black man named James Cornish had been stabbed in the chest. He was in bad shape because the knife had sliced open his pericardium—the protective sack around the heart. At that time, heart surgery was incredibly risky, and few surgeons would attempt it. Using his advanced sterilization techniques and every ounce of his courage, Dr. Williams opened Cornish's chest and proceeded to do what had never been done before in Chicago—and maybe only once before anywhere in the modern world: He sutured (stitched up) the heart sack, closed up the incision, and watched his patient recover. James Cornish left the hospital and went on to live for decades more. This is generally considered to be the world's first successful heart surgery.

The next year, Dr. Williams was invited to serve as chief surgeon at Freedmen's Hospital in Washington, D.C. There he continued to push the boundaries of surgery. He also never stopped advocating for the advancement of African-American physicians and nurses. In 1895, he co-founded the National Medical Association, the first professional organization for medical practitioners that allowed African-American members.

> "Anything is possible, when it is done in love, and everything you can do should be in love or it will fail."
> —Daniel Hale Williams

ROYAL RUNDOWN

⇒ **BORN:** January 18, 1856, Hollidaysburg, Pennsylvania, U.S.A. ⇒ **DIED:** August 4, 1931, Idlewild, Michigan, U.S.A. ⇒ **LED:** Heart surgery ⇒ **REMEMBERED FOR:** Starting the first African-American-owned-and-operated hospital in America and advocating for African Americans in medical fields

Civil rights leaders, including Martin Luther King, Jr. (center), during the 1963 March on Washington for Jobs and Freedom

STRENGTH IN **NUMBERS**

FIT FOR A KING

Dr. Martin Luther King, Jr., was a powerful, inspirational leader—undeniably one of the most important figures in the American civil rights movement. King spent his life standing up to racism, fighting for equal rights for African Americans, and advocating for peaceful protest against unjust laws. But a movement takes more than one man, and one of the hallmarks of great leadership is the ability to inspire and work with others to create change. Here are just a few of the many influential people who worked alongside King to make the movement a success.

CLEVELAND ROBINSON

A respected leader in New York City's labor unions, Cleveland Robinson fought to give tens of thousands of minority workers a voice in their places of work. Furthermore, Robinson helped African Americans become leaders inside America's biggest labor union advocate, the American Federation of Labor and Congress of Industrial Organizations (AFL-CIO). His passion and skills led him to become an adviser to King on important economic issues.

During the civil rights movement, King and others asked people to stand up for their rights. But many didn't understand what their rights were in the first place. That's where Dorothy Cotton came in. A crucial—but often overlooked—part of King's team, Cotton worked tirelessly to educate others about protesting, organizing, and exercising their civil rights. She led a program that taught thousands of African Americans how to register to vote and to participate in government.

BAYARD RUSTIN

Bayard Rustin made a huge impact on the movement as King's behind-the-scenes guy, helping to organize the logistics of peaceful protests and even the massive March on Washington. An openly gay man in the 1960s, Rustin was often misunderstood and shrouded in controversy. Despite the prejudice he encountered, he remained a courageous advocate for peace and equality for all, as well as one of King's most trusted advisers.

JOHN LEWIS

First inspired as a kid after hearing King speak on the radio, John Lewis became an influential figure at a young age. As a college student, he risked his life to protest segregation and organize other students to do the same. At only 23 years old, he spoke to more than 200,000 people at the March on Washington for Jobs and Freedom—the same event where King gave his famous "I Have a Dream" speech. Lewis didn't stop there: Since the 1980s, he's served in Congress, where he's continued to fight for civil rights in the United States. In 2011, President Barack Obama awarded him the Presidential Medal of Freedom—the country's highest civilian honor.

Astronaut Eugene A. Cernan, the last person to walk on the moon to date, rides the Lunar Roving Vehicle during the Apollo 17 mission in 1972.

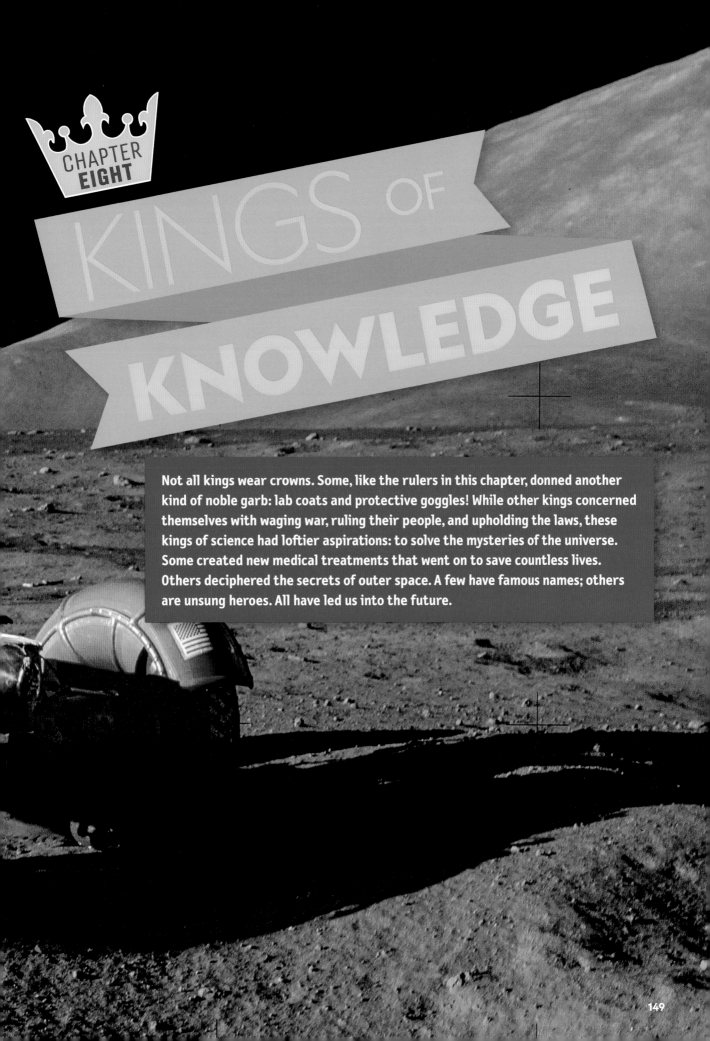

KINGS OF KNOWLEDGE

Not all kings wear crowns. Some, like the rulers in this chapter, donned another kind of noble garb: lab coats and protective goggles! While other kings concerned themselves with waging war, ruling their people, and upholding the laws, these kings of science had loftier aspirations: to solve the mysteries of the universe. Some created new medical treatments that went on to save countless lives. Others deciphered the secrets of outer space. A few have famous names; others are unsung heroes. All have led us into the future.

ISAAC NEWTON

⟽ KING OF PHYSICS ⟾

O ur understanding of the world around us has been built by countless hardworking scientists doing their part. Every once in a while, one of them shifts the whole process of discovery into overdrive. Isaac Newton was one of those people.

NEWTON AND THE APPLE TREE

Generations of schoolchildren have been taught the same tale about how the legendary scientist discovered gravity: A young Newton is sitting underneath an apple tree, thinking about the universe when—*boink!*—an apple falls, hitting him on the head. In an instant, Newton realizes that the same force that made the apple fall is also the one that keeps the moon close to Earth and Earth close to the sun: gravity.

It's one of the most famous stories in the history of science, but it's not exactly true: Newton himself wrote that his interest in gravity was sparked when he watched an apple fall—but it didn't hit him. The event occurred during an 18-month period when Newton's college, the University of Cambridge, was closed due to plague. It was during this time that Newton came up with the foundations of many of his most important ideas. In 1687, they were published as the *Principia*—often said to be the single most influential book on physics in history.

> "If I have seen further it is by standing on the shoulders of giants."
> —Isaac Newton

ROYAL RUNDOWN

➤➤ **BORN:** January 4, 1643, Woolsthorpe-by-Colsterworth, England   ➤➤ **DIED:** March 31, 1727, London, England   ➤➤ **LED:** The Royal Society of London   ➤➤ **REMEMBERED FOR:** The laws of motion that are the foundation of physics

UNLOCKING THE UNIVERSE

In the book, Newton laid out his three basic laws of motion, which explain how objects move. Using his own laws, Newton also came up with his theory of gravity. Together, his ideas explain not only how and why apples fall from trees but also how the planets and moons of the solar system move around each other.

Newton realized that his new laws made it possible to calculate the mass of each planet and explain the tides—so he did that, too. And when the mathematics of the time fell short in describing the motion of the planets, Newton simply invented a new kind of math: calculus. Newton's ideas gave modern science the keys to unlock how the universe worked.

In 1703, he was elected president of London's Royal Society, the world's oldest and most prestigious scientific organization. But though he was undeniably brilliant, Newton wasn't loved by everyone.

A SHARP MIND

Famously antisocial and egotistical, Newton rubbed a lot of people the wrong way. He had no fewer than three fierce rivalries with other scientists of his day. The first was English astronomer John Flamsteed, who let Newton borrow his notes on the motion of the moon on the condition that they were for his personal use only. But Newton broke his word and published the notes without permission. He also feuded with German mathematician Gottfried Leibniz over who deserved the credit for inventing calculus. (Today, historians agree that the two men arrived at the idea independently.) And Newton used his power as president of the Royal Society to wipe a competitor in his work on gravity, Robert Hooke, out of the history books.

Prickly personality aside, Isaac Newton is undoubtedly one of the greatest scientific minds there has ever been. Besides discovering gravity, writing the laws of motion, and inventing calculus, he also constructed the world's first reflecting telescope and made groundbreaking discoveries in the field of optics: asserting that light was made of particles and that white light was a combination of all the colors of the rainbow. Today, he's remembered as a scientist who forever changed the way we make sense of the forces that shape our universe.

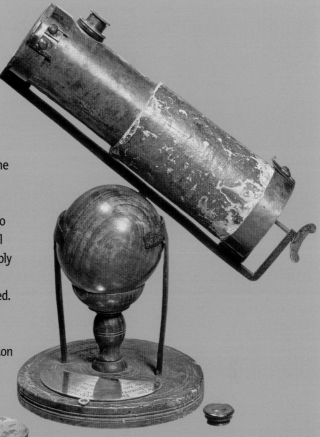

A telescope belonging to Isaac Newton, circa 1671

COMMANDING QUEENS

QUEEN OF REASON
Hypatia (A.D. 355–415)

Long before Newton, another mathematician really shook things up: Hypatia, the first known female mathematician in history and the leading mathematician of her time. She lived in Alexandria, Egypt, in the fourth century A.D., where she lectured on math, astronomy, and philosophy. Although none of her writings have survived, some scholars believe she was responsible for ideas about the stars and planets that were not overturned until the time of Galileo, 1,200 years later. She did work in algebra and probably assisted with the invention of the astrolabe, a device for measuring the altitude of stars and planets. As a pagan in a time of religious strife, Hypatia was eventually murdered by a religious mob. Since then, she has stood as a symbol of science and reason.

SCIENCE'S
DYNAMIC DUOS

Partners in Learning and Reason

Many scientists work shoulder-to-shoulder with other scientists, teaming up to pool resources and to build on each other's ideas. Others work independently on the same problems. And still others are fierce competitors, elbowing each other aside to be the first to reach a common goal. Here are some of science's most famous pairs.

COMPUTER CO-KINGS:
Jack Kilby & Robert Noyce

The first computers were truly huge. Just one of these beasts loomed nine feet (3 m) tall and weighed as much as a dinosaur! Fortunately, in the 1950s, two men were simultaneously working on a way to miniaturize these massive machines. The first to finish the world-changing project was Jack Kilby, who invented integrated circuits while working at American technology company Texas Instruments. These tiny pieces of technology replaced the massive vacuum tubes and sprawling systems of resistors, wires, and capacitors that made up the "brains" of the early machines. Kilby did it first, but Robert Noyce—who was working independently for his own company, Fairchild Semiconductor—managed to create an even better version of the circuit built into a single chip of silicon. For his innovation, Kilby received the Nobel Prize in physics in 2000. Noyce went on to reap rewards of a different kind: as a co-founder of technology company Intel, one of the world's leading manufacturers of computer parts.

Robert Noyce
(top) and
Jack Kilby

SURGERY SIDEKICKS: Vivien Thomas & Alfred Blalock

Just 60 years ago, heart surgery was considered so dangerous that many doctors would not attempt it. But one, Alfred Blalock, was determined to find a way to fix a certain heart condition affecting newborns. In 1944, he stepped up to the operating table and carefully connected two arteries to increase blood flow to his patient's heart. With this groundbreaking technique, he saved his patient's life and countless others after that. But Blalock didn't invent the life-saving procedure he had performed: It was the brainchild of Vivien Thomas, his African-American surgical technician. Thomas supervised the surgical laboratories at Johns Hopkins University for 35 years, developing groundbreaking techniques and surgical equipment. But because he was an African-American man working in a time of extreme racial bias, Thomas did not receive recognition for his innovations until 1976, when he was appointed an instructor of surgery and awarded an honorary degree.

Vivien Thomas (top)
and Alfred Blalock

DAREDEVIL DOCTORS:
Barry Marshall & Robin Warren

Before the 1980s, one in 10 adults was struck by an incredibly painful—and sometimes lethal—condition: stomach ulcers, painful sores that develop in the lining of the stomach. Most physicians were certain that ulcers were caused by stress and lifestyle choices. But Barry Marshall, an Australian doctor, believed the accepted medical wisdom was wrong. He teamed up with Australian pathologist Robin Warren, and the two discovered something remarkable: Every single ulcer patient they studied was infected with a bacteria called *Helicobacter pylori*. When the two scientists announced that they believed the bacteria was causing ulcers, the medical community laughed them off. So in 1984, Marshall did something drastic: He drank a flask of *H. pylori* ... and gave himself terrible ulcers! Marshall took antibiotics and—just as he predicted he would—he cured himself. Since then, ulcers have become a simple medical problem to treat. For their discovery, and for their incredible bravery, Marshall and Warren shared the 2005 Nobel Prize in medicine.

Barry Marshall (left) and Robin Warren

EMPERORS OF EVOLUTION:
Charles Darwin & Alfred Russel Wallace

Much can be discovered from the beak of a bird. After Charles Darwin ventured to the Galápagos Islands in 1835, he realized that the various birds on the islands, all coming from the same ancestor, were indeed different species. Their physical features, like beaks, had altered from one to the other so each species could eat certain types of foods in its respective location. Twenty years later in the Dutch East Indies, current-day Indonesia, Alfred Russel Wallace reached similar conclusions: Animals change and adapt to their environment in order to survive. The two British biologists together offered a presentation in 1858 putting forth the theory of evolution by natural selection—that living things possessing traits that allow them to better adapt to their environment than other members of their species will be more likely to survive and pass along their genes to their offspring. Over the course of many generations, as traits become more or less common, a species evolves. Darwin published his famous book *On the Origin of Species* the following year, but Wallace—despite a distinguished scientific career both before and after the 1858 collaboration with Darwin—never himself became a household name.

Charles Darwin (left) and
Alfred Russel Wallace

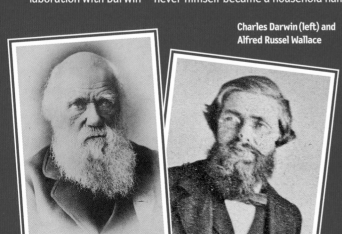

CHANGING THE COURSE OF SCIENCE
Marie Curie (1867–1934)

COMMANDING QUEENS

Marie Skłodowska was born in 1867 in Warsaw, Poland, where she lived until she moved to France in 1891 to continue her scientific studies. There, she met her future husband, Pierre Curie, and together they started working to research the invisible rays given off by the element uranium. Pierre was tragically killed in an accident on a Paris street in 1906, but Marie continued with her research. She developed a way to measure radioactivity as well as a mobile x-ray unit that was first used during World War I to assist wounded soldiers.

Pierre and Marie Curie

Curie was the first woman to win a Nobel Prize, awarded to her and Pierre, in 1903, for their research on radiation. She's also the only woman (so far) to win two: She was awarded her second Nobel Prize in 1911, for her discoveries and studies of the elements radium and polonium. Her hard work and success furthered the goal of women being treated as equals among their male colleagues—and she continues to inspire young scientists today.

STEVE WOZNIAK

THE INVENTOR

Steve Wozniak grew up enchanted by science fiction. He was especially enthralled with the technology that characters would use, like universal translators and watches that made phone calls. At the time, these inventions were purely the stuff of sci-fi, but Wozniak loved to dream up ways about how to make them in real life.

He started experimenting with electronics, first with mail-order kits with step-by-step instructions. Eventually, he built a device of his own invention: a house-to-house intercom he ran between his house and the houses of a few friends. It was the first time he had built something totally new—something that didn't already exist—but it was far from the last.

By the time he had graduated from high school, Wozniak was working on a far more complicated device: a kit computer that would eventually become known as the Apple I. Hewlett-Packard, where Wozniak worked as an intern at the time, wasn't interested in the device. So instead, Wozniak and his friend Steve Jobs went their own way, founding the Apple Computer Company in 1976. Wozniak was in charge of the engineering, and Jobs was in charge of marketing. When a local store ordered 50 preassembled computers, the two thought they might have a hit on their hands.

In 1977, Wozniak created the Apple II, which had color graphics and came in a case with a built-in keyboard. It revolutionized the computer industry: By 1983, the company was worth $985 million. Wozniak's contributions to personal computing were recognized by the highest office in the land in 1985, when he and Jobs received the National Medal of Technology. Today, Wozniak is a philanthropist and advocate for technological advancements. He still loves sci-fi.

> "If you love what you do and are willing to do what it takes, it's within your reach."
> —Steve Wozniak

ROYAL RUNDOWN

➞ **BORN:** August 11, 1950, San Jose, California, U.S.A. ➞ **LEADS:** Personal computers
➞ **KNOWN FOR:** Founding Apple and engineering a computer that revolutionized the technology industry

STEVE JOBS

THE BUSINESSMAN

When he was growing up in Mountain View, California, U.S.A., Steve Jobs loved to take apart and rebuild electronics in the garage with his father, a machinist. In high school, he was brave enough to call up Hewlett-Packard president William Hewlett and ask him for some parts for a class project. Impressed, Hewlett gave him the parts—and a summer internship, too. It was there that Jobs met Steve Wozniak and developed a friendship that would change the world.

Jobs was a brilliant businessman with a knack for understanding what the public wanted. With Jobs at the helm, Apple Computer Company became a tremendous success: Its first personal computer, the Apple II, was easy to use, and it earned three million dollars in the first year alone. But Jobs wasn't an easy person to work with. He was impatient and could be a bit of a bully. In 1983, he was ousted from Apple's board of directors, and in 1985, Jobs sold all his Apple stock and resigned.

With his newfound free time, Jobs turned to other ventures. He bankrolled a small animation studio that came to be known as Pixar. Jobs cut a deal with Disney and produced the first ever computer-animated feature film. That movie was *Toy Story,* and it was a smash hit when it was released in 1995.

In 1997, Apple's board of directors was desperate. The company was in such bad shape it was no longer profitable. So they made a radical decision: They asked Jobs to come back. Over the next decade, Jobs used his vigor and talent for design to turn Apple around. Since the introduction of the iPhone in 2007, Apple has spent time on top of the list of America's most valuable companies—not bad for a company started by a couple of guys in a garage!

"I want to put a ding in the universe."
—*Steve Jobs*

ROYAL RUNDOWN

BORN: February 24, 1955, San Francisco, California, U.S.A. **DIED:** October 5, 2011, Palo Alto, California, U.S.A. **LED:** Computing gadgets **REMEMBERED FOR:** Founding Apple and introducing the world to groundbreaking technologies

EMPERORS OF EXPLORATION

They Left No Stone Unturned

These fearless explorers traveled the world in search of adventure, taking risks in the name of research and discovery. They made their way to the remote and uncharted corners of Earth, and what they found, whether it was an ancient tomb or a long-lost city, changed our understanding of human history.

PATHFINDER TO THE PHARAOHS:
Howard Carter (1874–1939)

A skilled artist and a man of constant curiosity, British archaeologist Howard Carter was drawn into the investigation of ancient civilizations starting at a young age. He joined an archaeological survey of Egypt at age 17, where he helped unearth and explore the tombs of Hatshepsut, Amenhotep, and several other pharaohs, or Egyptian kings.

His most famed discovery was the mostly untouched tomb of King Tutankhamun. In November 1922, Carter and his team stumbled upon what turned out to be a staircase covered in debris. They spent weeks of clearing away sand and gravel, at last uncovering the top of a doorway sealed with plaster. After opening the tomb, Carter saw glittering gold everywhere he looked: chariots, chairs, chests, beads, life-size figures, and a throne. He made his way to the burial chamber and unpacked several coffins to come across the untouched mummy of Tutankhamun himself, adorned with a glistening golden funerary mask. With those findings, Carter brought to life the mysterious 18th dynasty of ancient Egypt, and made King Tut, a boy king who ruled for only nine years, a worldwide sensation and a household name.

REAL-LIFE INDIANA JONES:
Hiram Bingham (1875–1956)

Hiram Bingham was a man of many accomplishments: He was a professor of Latin American history at Yale University and later became a U.S. governor and senator. But what many most remember him for is "discovering" the incredible Inca site we know as Machu Picchu (p. 21).

Bingham, who was seeking the "lost city of the Incas," was led to the site in 1911 by a local guide who shepherded

KING OF HUMAN EVOLUTION:
Louis Leakey (1903–1972)

Where do we come from? It's a question that has fascinated humans for thousands of years, and it was the life's work of Louis Leakey. A paleo-anthropologist—scientist who studies human fossils—he brought the study of human origins into the public eye. Born in Kenya, Africa, to missionary parents, Leakey found his first artifacts—ancient stone tools—as a teenager. That discovery helped convince him that Africa was the birthplace of humankind, a notion that most people at the time didn't think was true. But Leakey made proving it his mission. Along the way, he teamed up with his archaeologist wife, Mary Leakey, and the two made one incredible discovery after another: One of their most famous was early fossils of an ancient species of human, *Homo habilis*, which walked across Africa about two million years ago.

KING OF THE SEA:
Robert Ballard (1942–)

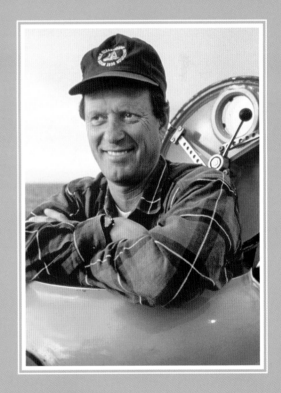

As one of the world's foremost deep-sea explorers, Robert Ballard spends many of his workdays peering through the portal of a submarine. He is most famous for being the man who in 1985 discovered the wreck of the *Titanic*, the infamous passenger liner that sunk on its maiden voyage after striking an iceberg in 1912. What many people *don't* know is that Ballard wasn't supposed to be looking for *Titanic* during that operation at all; he had been commissioned by the United States Navy to investigate two lost nuclear submarines, the U.S.S. *Scorpion* and the U.S.S. *Thresher,* both of which he found.

But the crown jewel of Ballard's ocean discoveries has been one that has nothing to do with ships at all. In 1977, he was the first explorer to find hydrothermal vents on the ocean floor—geological wonders that create zones of blistering, super-heated water around them. In the process, they sustain previously unthinkable ecosystems of chemical-eating bacteria, tube worms, and other life-forms that manage to survive conditions once thought too extreme for living things. Ballard's was one of the most important biological discoveries of the modern age.

Bingham and his team through dense tropical forests, across bridges made of tree trunks, and on treks up towering mountains. What Bingham beheld high in the Andes Mountains, about 50 miles (80 km) northwest of Cusco, Peru, was worth the quest: a remarkably well-preserved, nearly intact ancient site that contained impressive stonework, pottery, jewelry, kitchen utensils, steep staircases, and burial sites. His study of this treasure of ancient history and his articles in *National Geographic* magazine spurred future interest and archaeological discoveries in Latin America. It also made him one of the key inspirations for the most famed fictional adventure-archaeologist on the big screen: Indiana Jones.

MOON WALKERS

◄══ LORDS OF THE LUNAR SURFACE ══▌•○

People have stared at the moon since ancient times and wondered what it would be like to visit that glowing orb in the night sky. We finally found out on July 20, 1969, when Neil Armstrong and Buzz Aldrin became the first humans to walk on the lunar surface. Only 10 astronauts have since followed in their footsteps. The trip took guts, grit, and determination—but these men had the right stuff.

NEIL ARMSTRONG (1930–2012)

Hometown: Wapakoneta, Ohio, U.S.A.
Moonwalking Mission: Apollo 11 (1969)
Fun Fact: 600 million people watched him walk on the moon on TV.

EDWIN "BUZZ" ALDRIN, JR. (1930–)

Hometown: Montclair, New Jersey, U.S.A.
Moonwalking Mission: Apollo 11 (1969)
Fun Fact: He helped pioneer underwater training to get astronauts ready to go to space.

CHARLES "PETE" CONRAD (1930–1999)

Hometown: Philadelphia, Pennsylvania, U.S.A.
Moonwalking Mission: Apollo 12 (1969)
Fun Fact: He captained the lunar module in the second moon landing.

ALAN L. BEAN (1932–2018)

Hometown: Wheeler, Texas, U.S.A.
Moonwalking Mission: Apollo 12 (1969)
Fun Fact: In 1981, he retired from NASA to become an artist.

ALAN SHEPARD (1923–1998)

Hometown: East Derry, New Hampshire, U.S.A.
Moonwalking Mission: Apollo 14 (1971)
Fun Fact: On February 6, 1971, he smuggled a golf club onto the moon and hit two balls. In the low-gravity environment, they went miles!

ED MITCHELL (1930–2016)

Hometown: Artesia, New Mexico, U.S.A.
Moonwalking Mission: Apollo 14 (1971)
Fun Fact: He helped bring nearly 100 pounds (45 kg) of moon rocks back to Earth for scientific study.

Astronaut Alan L. Bean, lunar module pilot for the Apollo 12 lunar landing mission

DAVID SCOTT (1932–)

Hometown: San Antonio, Texas, U.S.A.
Moonwalking Mission: Apollo 15 (1971)
Fun Fact: He was the first person to drive the lunar rover vehicle on the moon.

JAMES B. IRWIN (1930–1991)

Hometown: Pittsburgh, Pennsylvania, U.S.A.
Moonwalking Mission: Apollo 15 (1971)
Fun Fact: Going to the moon was Irwin's childhood dream—and he was the eighth person to do it.

JOHN YOUNG (1930–2018)

Hometown: San Francisco, California, U.S.A.
Moonwalking Mission: Apollo 16 (1972)
Fun Fact: He was NASA's longest-serving astronaut, with a career spanning 42 years.

CHARLES MOSS DUKE, JR. (1935–)

Hometown: Charlotte, North Carolina, U.S.A.
Moonwalking Mission: Apollo 16 (1972)
Fun Fact: From the ground, he helped guide the crew of Apollo 11 on the first moon landing.

HARRISON "JACK" SCHMITT (1935–)

Hometown: Santa Rita, New Mexico, U.S.A.
Moonwalking Mission: Apollo 17 (1972)
Fun Fact: Schmitt, a geologist, was the first trained scientist on the moon.

EUGENE A. CERNAN (1934–2017)

Hometown: Chicago, Illinois, U.S.A.
Moonwalking Mission: Apollo 17 (1972)
Fun Fact: He was the last person to walk on the moon to date.

THE MISSING MISSION: APOLLO 13

You might have noticed that the moon missions on this page skipped from Apollo 12 to Apollo 14. What happened to Apollo 13? This spaceflight was a near disaster—but through quick thinking and teamwork, it became one of NASA's finest hours.

Apollo 13 was two days into its mission to the moon, about 205,000 miles (328,915 km) from Earth, when something went wrong. Its astronauts heard a loud bang—the sound of an exploding oxygen tank. The three crew members—Jim Lovell, Fred Haise, and Jack Swigert—looked out the spacecraft window to see the oxygen they depended on to breathe and for fuel leaking out into space. In an instant, flight controllers across the United States sprang into action. Over four days, they made a series of complex, high-pressure choices to try to save the crew's lives. When they realized the problem couldn't be fixed, they made a daring decision: To have a chance at survival, the three-man crew would have to bundle into the two-man lunar module that was meant to land on the moon.

The lunar module had enough oxygen but not enough water, and its systems weren't designed to filter enough air for three astronauts over several days. Engineers on the ground figured out how to use a mishmash of supplies aboard Apollo 13—including the flight manual cover and a pair of socks—to reconfigure the module into a "lifeboat" capable of carrying the astronauts back to Earth. Throughout the four-day ordeal, the crew and flight controllers never lost their cool. And on April 17, 1970, Lovell, Haise, and Swigert safely splashed down in the Pacific Ocean. Though they never made it to the moon, in that moment, they—and the thousands of flight controllers that helped them from Earth—became heroes all the same.

CARL SAGAN

⟨══ KING OF THE COSMOS ══⟩●

Few scientists become celebrities. Many are content to remain far from the public eye, peering down into microscopes or up into telescopes. Astronomer Carl Sagan was different. He loved his work so much that he found his greatest passion was sharing it with the world. Through books and television programs, Sagan harnessed the power of media to bring the universe to the living rooms of millions of Americans.

When Sagan was a young scientist, in the 1960s, the field of planetary science was in its infancy. NASA was still preparing to put a man on the moon, and it had yet to send out probes to the rest of the solar system. Everything known about the universe had to be deduced from telescopes. Sagan was interested in what conditions were like on other planets, correctly predicting that Venus was incredibly hot and that dust storms swept the surface of Mars.

Sagan helped develop sensors for NASA's Mariner 2, the first probe sent to the planet Venus. It was during those missions that he discovered a hidden skill: He had a knack for talking to reporters about the work he and other NASA scientists were doing. Sagan could explain the science in a way that made it seem understandable—and even beautiful—to the American public.

In 1977, NASA embarked on an ambitious project: It launched twin probes, Voyager 1 and Voyager 2, to explore the outer planets: Jupiter, then Saturn, then—if the spacecraft lasted that long—Uranus and Neptune. (Those probes, which were only supposed to last four years, are still going today. One of

> "Somewhere, something incredible is waiting to be known."
> —*Carl Sagan*

ROYAL RUNDOWN

➤➤ **BORN:** November 9, 1934, Brooklyn, New York, U.S.A. ➤➤ **DIED:** December 20, 1996, Seattle, Washington, U.S.A. ➤➤ **LED:** Astronomy ➤➤ **REMEMBERED FOR:** Bringing science to the people

them, Voyager 1, has become the first man-made object to leave the solar system and explore interstellar space.)

Sagan chaired a NASA committee tasked with preparing a special piece of cargo that would ride on the Voyager crafts into the great unknown: the "Golden Record." Meant to describe life on Earth to any spacefaring aliens that might find them, the two copies of the Golden Record contain images of the solar system, DNA, and human anatomy, along with nature sounds and greetings in 55 languages. The Golden Record also contains all kinds of music, from classical to—at Sagan's insistence—the rock song "Johnny B. Goode" by Chuck Berry.

The Voyager craft carries the Golden Record (above), which contains images and sounds from Earth; an artist's impression of a Voyager flyby of the planet Saturn (left)

EXPLORER OF THE UNIVERSE

In the 1980s, Sagan's passion for astronomy rocketed him into fame. He co-wrote and narrated a 13-part TV miniseries called *Cosmos: A Personal Voyage.* It became the most popular thing to ever air on American public television at the time. To date, it has been viewed by at least 500 million people in 60 countries. The series showcased Sagan's natural talent for explaining big-picture ideas in a way that anyone could understand, and his enthusiasm was infectious. The show made him a full-blown pop-culture icon and inspired millions of people to fall in love with the science of the universe.

Sagan would ride his rising star into the world of science fiction with his 1985 novel *Contact.* That book allowed him to write about something that had been on his mind ever since he first peered through a telescope: Is there anyone looking back? His novel, which later became a hit 1997 film, asked questions about what might happen in the events following first contact between humans and extraterrestrials.

Today, Sagan is fondly remembered as the man who brought science to the masses. He inspired a generation of not only young scientists but also regular people to look up at the stars and wonder.

QUEEN OF THE SOLAR SYSTEM
Claudia Alexander
(1959–2015)

In a field where nearly everyone was a white man, Claudia Alexander stood out. But not only because she was a woman of color: Alexander was a brilliant scientist who changed what we know about our solar system and a leader whose love of learning inspired everyone around her. After a high school internship with NASA that fostered her love of space science and a 1993 doctorate in plasma physics from the University of Michigan, she joined NASA's Galileo mission to study Jupiter. With Alexander at the helm, the mission discovered 21 moons, revealed Jupiter's atmosphere for the first time, and discovered an atmosphere on the moon Ganymede. Alexander also worked on the European Space Agency's Rosetta mission, a 10-year project to study and land on a comet, which it did in 2014. She shared her infectious love for her work, writing not only scientific papers but also children's books and science fiction.

MONARCHS OF THE GREAT OUTDOORS

Planetary Protectors

A good king strives to protect his kingdom and to keep it safe and sound. These awesome environmentalists—kings of the natural world—dedicated their lives to defending Mother Nature.

BARON OF BIRDS:
John James Audubon (1785–1851)

In 1803, John James Audubon's father sent him away from his home of Nantes, France, to America with a fake passport to avoid being drafted into Napoleon's army. The young Audubon found himself with lots of time on his hands and not much to do in the woods of Pennsylvania, so he spent his late teens hunting and observing the natural world. Audubon was especially interested in birds and, eventually, traveled all the way from Florida to Labrador, Canada, writing his observations of birds in the wild and painting pictures to go alongside them. He published 453 of these drawings in his famous *Birds of America*, printed between 1827 and 1838. The work was so influential that it was quoted by Charles Darwin, the father of the theory of the evolution of species . Today, the largest version of the work ever produced is considered the most valuable printed book in the world. His legacy lives on with the National Audubon Society, an organization that protects birds and their habitats around the world.

KING OF THE WILDERNESS:
John Muir (1838–1914)

After nearly losing his sight in a factory accident as a young man, John Muir resolved to spend his life admiring the beauty of the natural world. He moved out west, far from industrial America, and spent years hiking in and around the future site of Yosemite National Park—an education he called the "University of the Wilderness." Muir began publishing articles and essays urging people to be more responsible with America's land. He was one of the first people to pioneer the idea of creating protected areas to keep wild lands wild. Muir personally led U.S. president Theodore Roosevelt around places that went on to become protected parks, such as Yosemite, Sequoia, and the Grand Canyon. He also formed the Sierra Club, an environmental group dedicated to the preservation of America's natural beauty for future generations of campers, hikers, and explorers.

VOICE OF THE PLANET:
David Attenborough (1926–)

His iconic voice has brought to life the dances of jungle birds, the deadly fights between lions and antelopes, and the magical world of coral reefs. David Attenborough was fascinated with the natural world as a young boy, collecting bird eggs and fossils he found outside. After earning his degree in the natural sciences from the University of Cambridge, in Cambridge, England, Attenborough went to work as a television producer. In 1954, he launched a series called *Zoo Quest*, the first of many nature documentaries he would create for the British Broadcasting Corporation (BBC). Since then, Attenborough has devoted his life to sharing his delight at the beauty and wonder of nature. He's been the voice of the iconic nature series *Planet Earth*, and he's been so influential in raising awareness for environmental conservation that scientists have named more than 15 species for him. And while Attenborough isn't technically a king, he is a real-life knight! He received the honor from Her Majesty the Queen of England in 1985 for his service to the people and the planet we all rely on.

FEARLESS NATURALIST:
Minakata Kumagusu (1867–1941)

While some call Japanese naturalist Minakata Kumagusu "eccentric," the word that best describes him is "fearless." Though he never got a university degree, he made the world his classroom instead. At the age of 19, he went to explore the woods of a distant, foreign land: Michigan, U.S.A. As a young man, he went on to travel all over the United States, eventually making his way to the Caribbean, where he joined a traveling circus, collecting rare and undocumented species of slime molds and other fungi along the way. In 1892, Kumagusu set sail for Britain, where he came to international fame for his publications in the scientific journal *Nature*. After a 14-year odyssey abroad, Kumagusu returned to Japan and became the country's leading environmentalist. Through protest and activism, he managed to save several forests and even establish the island of Kashima as a natural monument.

COMMANDING QUEENS

GREEN QUEEN
Wangari Maathai
(1940–2011)

Born in Kenya, Wangari Maathai was the first woman in East and Central Africa to earn a doctorate degree, in 1971. But her extraordinary career was just beginning. At the time, Kenya's forests were being devastated as trees were cut down to make way for buildings. Maathai thought that if she could gather women together to plant trees across Kenya, she could help fight deforestation and create jobs for women at the same time. Not everyone was a fan of Maathai's ideas: She was teargassed by police and thrown in jail for leading protests. But her organization, the Green Belt Movement, grew to become one of the largest grassroots movements in Africa from its founding in 1977, gathering nearly 900,000 women to plant more than 30 million trees. In 2004, Maathai was awarded the Nobel Peace Prize for her fight to help the environment.

NIZAR IBRAHIM

═◄ DESERT DETECTIVE ═┥○

In 1911, a German paleontologist named Ernst Stromer made an incredible discovery in the Egyptian desert: a fossil of a large, meat-eating animal with long jaws and a sail-like structure on its back. He named the animal *Spinosaurus aegyptiacus* and took it to a museum in Munich, Germany—which was later bombed during an air raid toward the end of World War II. Almost all of Stromer's fossils were destroyed—leaving only his field notes and drawings to tell the story of his discovery.

About a century later, in 2008, a young German paleontologist named Nizar Ibrahim set out to rediscover the beast in the searing sands of the Sahara. Spotting an incredibly large fossil embedded in a steep hillside, Ibrahim and his team stopped to check it out. They didn't have any of the supplies needed to excavate a huge, 100-million-year-old bone, but with a little ingenuity—and a rushed 100-mile (161-km) drive into the nearest town—the team was successful. Any other dino hunter would have been thrilled, but the bone belonged to a plant-eating dinosaur, not the colossal predator Ibrahim had hoped to find.

After several more years of combing the desert, Ibrahim and his team struck paleontology gold: They were able to track down a dig site where a local fossil hunter had found several bones belonging to *Spinosaurus*. Judging from the bones, Ibrahim thinks that *Spinosaurus*—a predator around 15 feet (4.6 m) longer than *Tyrannosaurus rex*, a dino previously believed to be the largest land predator of the Cretaceous period—spent at least part of its life in the water, making it the only true dinosaur adapted to life in the rivers that once flowed across the Sahara. He also believes it is the largest predatory dinosaur to have roamed Earth.

Spinosaurus could be considered a once-in-a-lifetime discovery. But Ibrahim—who has also uncovered the remains of flying reptiles, croc-like hunters, turtles, snakes, fish, and more—has only just begun sifting through the sands of North Africa in the hope of solving more mysteries of the dinosaurs.

> "I think the Sahara's still full of treasures."
> —Nizar Ibrahim

ROYAL RUNDOWN

➤ **BORN:** September 8, 1982, Berlin, Germany ➤ **LEADS:** Cretaceous paleontology
➤ **KNOWN FOR:** Discovering the largest predatory dinosaur ever found

DONG ZHIMING

⊶═ MR. DINOSAR ═⊷

What's the best part about discovering a new dinosaur? Is it the excitement of discovery? The fame? Or maybe it's getting to name the ancient beast that once walked Earth?

Chinese paleontologist Dong Zhiming has discovered many new dinosaurs and given them some very creative names. Some, like the Jurassic-period plant-eater *Datousaurus*, he named after the animal's physical characteristics. (*Dàtóu* is the Chinese word for "big head.") Others, like the two-legged carnivore *Gasosaurus*, he's named with a little more humor: This dino's remains were found through the reports of workers at a gas mining company.

Dubbed "China's Mr. Dinosaur" by a *National Geographic* science editor, Zhiming is celebrated for putting China in paleontology's spotlight. Since his first big discovery of a gargantuan sauropod (a long-necked plant-eater) in 1963, Zhiming has wowed fellow dinosaur hunters with the pace at which he finds fossils. He has been particularly successful in the rural country of northwest China, where he discovered that traditional folk medicine practiced there sometimes involved grinding up "dragon bone." Zhiming had a hunch that what the locals were really crushing was dinosaur fossils—and he was right.

Zhiming is especially famous for excavating sites dating to the Middle Jurassic period, which lasted from about 174 to 163 million years ago. At the time, few dinosaur fossils from this era had been found anywhere in the world—but Zhiming found that China had a wealth of them. At one site, Dashanpu, he has found a "dinosaur graveyard," where all kinds of species lay together, possibly wiped out by an ancient Jurassic flood. There were huge stegosaurs, two-legged plant-eaters, and pterodactyls. In 1987, a museum opened on the site, bringing these ancient beasts back to life—all thanks to Mr. Dinosaur.

Zhiming has discovered an astounding 18 new dinosaur genera, or groups of species.

ROYAL RUNDOWN

➼ **BORN:** January 1937, Weihai, China ➼ **LEADS:** Jurassic paleontology
➼ **KNOWN FOR:** Discovering new dinosaur species, drawing attention to Chinese paleontology

FIT FOR A KING

DARE TO EXPLORE

From plummeting 24 miles (39 km) from space to Earth to flying solo around the world, these National Geographic extreme adventurers break records, explore uncharted territories, and push through obstacles in every part of the world.

FELIX BAUMGARTNER

Jumping off a skateboard-size platform in space to free-fall more than 24 miles (39 km) to Earth may sound like a nightmare for some. But for Austrian base jumper Felix Baumgartner, the nine-minute feat was the rush of a lifetime. Though he was equipped with a state-of-the-art pressurized space suit and parachute, the safety of the jump was anything but guaranteed. During his legendary leap, the daredevil of skydiving nearly spun out of control, but he stabilized himself and reached a speed of 843.6 miles an hour (1,357.6 km/h), becoming the first human to break the sound barrier without help from a machine.

BARRINGTON IRVING

At 23 years old, Barrington Irving was the youngest person and the first African American to fly solo around the world! After his legendary 97-day journey, Irving was inspired to give kids the same opportunities he had to learn about science and aviation. He created Experience Aviation, a nonprofit organization that provides hands-on STEM-focused education programs to underprivileged American students, often challenging them to design and build massive machines such as planes and sports cars.

YVES MOUSSALLAM

Descending into dangerous lava pits filled with blistering gases and scorching temperatures is just a part of Yves Moussallam's job. He is a volcanologist (a scientist who studies volcanoes), and it's his goal to understand how volcanic gas emissions, known as volcanic de-gassing, can help predict future volcanic activity, as well as how they will impact our atmosphere. In late 2015, he led a team of six other volcanologists on an incredible 10,500-mile (17,000-km) expedition across South America to measure gas emissions from 20 highly active volcanoes, some of which had never before been studied.

RAJESH **MAGAR**

Shooting down mountains at top speeds and swerving through rough terrain takes tremendous skill, guts, and dedication; Nepalese mountain biker Rajesh Magar possesses all those qualities. After teaching himself to ride a bike at the age of 10 and perfecting his craft by watching YouTube videos, Magar raced competitively using his "Franken-bike," which he altered using scraps and items found around town. This speedy superstar has now won several Nepalese national titles and awards all over Asia. But trophies and high stakes aside, this amazing athlete always enjoys the ride, saying, "mountain biking takes me to a place where I feel totally free."

MIKE **LIBECKI**

Extreme adventurer and California, U.S.A., native Mike Libecki is driven to explore, photograph, and often climb up the most remote, untouched places on the planet. One of his most recent feats involved trekking through rough terrain in Antarctica and Greenland, sometimes getting to these remote places on skis propelled by kites and sleeping on ledges 1,200 feet (366 m) off the ground. In one of his biggest accomplishments, Libecki and his climbing team braved blizzards, below-zero temperatures, blinding winds, and frostbite to become the first humans to summit Bertha's Tower in Antarctica.

STEVE **BOYES**

Hopping aboard traditional mokoro canoes, Boyes and his team weaved through waterways to complete a 1,500-mile (2,414-km) journey from Angola to Botswana. They were mapping—for the first time—the entire Okavango Delta, an enormous hub for wildlife biodiversity. The South African wildlife conservationist cataloged undocumented species, tested soil samples, and identified harmful human practices to understand how to best preserve this important ecosystem. His 121-day mission wasn't always smooth sailing, though. In addition to the team surviving broken bones, four canoe capsizes, and even a flesh-eating bacteria outbreak, a hippopotamus once charged and sank its tusks into the hull of Boyes's canoe!

YOUR TURN TO
WEAR THE CROWN

**Felix Baumgartner,
page 166**

Before you turned a page of *The Book of Kings*, you might've imagined that leading the royal life was a piece of cake: going to parties, making decrees, and having a court of people at the ready to meet your every whim. But as you've probably discovered, keeping power—and keeping people happy—is never an easy task.

The most remarkable rulers in history always led with thoughtfulness and respect. They wanted to hear the opinions of all the people—not just their appointed advisers. They weren't afraid to jump into the fray themselves and fight for the rights of their subjects, armed with their might or their voice. They were quick thinkers who were willing to take the helm at a moment's notice, always steering toward the future.

Maybe you have imagined yourself to be like a leader you read about. Nowadays, finding royals sitting on thrones with scepters and crowns is pretty rare. But that's no reason not to become a superstar sovereign of your own. Today, there are many different kinds of kings: kings who develop lifesaving technology, kings who write plays that make us laugh and cry, kings who find something they don't like about the world and do everything they can to change it for the better. Here are some kingly characteristics that all of history's most celebrated leaders have in common.

**Steve Jobs,
page 155**

**Saladin and Richard I,
pages 34–35**

Neil Armstrong,
page 158

1. KINGS
LEAD BY EXAMPLE.

The most honored kings don't just
expect their people to do good,
they lead by example and
are model citizens
themselves.

2. KINGS
ARE EAGER TO LEARN.

It's easy to get a big head when wearing a
colossal crown, but the most praised men
in history sought out advice and
reflected on their mistakes. They were
always striving to do better, and
they accepted help when they
needed it.

Martin Luther King, Jr.,
page 146

3. KINGS
MOTIVATE THE
MASSES.

A truly great ruler knows that his
real power rests in the hands of the
people. The mightiest men in history
inspired their people by listening to them,
by fostering the arts and sciences,
and by being open-minded to new
ideas, beliefs, and creative
solutions.

Pachacuti Inca Yupanqui,
page 20

4. KINGS
ARE CONFIDENT.

In order to have their people
believe in their decisions, these
daring dudes have to be
decisive. They are never
afraid to face
challenges.

5. KINGS
HAVE A
CLEAR VISION.

Remarkable rulers have well-
thought-out ideas of what they
want the future to look like, and
they pursue that vision with
persistence and passion.

T'Challa,
page 75

SO KEEP A GOOD GRIP
ON YOUR CROWN
AND SCEPTER.

Remember that with courage, an admirable
sense of fairness, and a heart set on making
the lives of others better, you too can
become a legendary leader who inspires
people, encourages positive change, and
makes the world a better place.

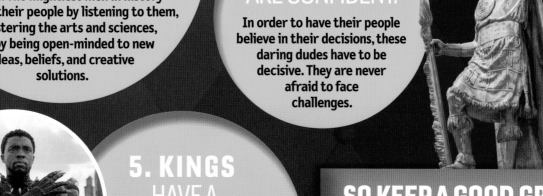

INDEX

Boldface indicates illustrations.

A

Abrams, J. J. 112
Abu Bakr (caliph) 24, **24**
Academy Awards (Oscars) 106–107, **106–107**
Achaemenid Empire 67, **67**
Action, aristocrats of 108–127
Actors
    Academy Awards (Oscars) 106–107, **106–107**
    action heroes 112–114, **112–114**
    Miranda, Lin-Manuel **5**, 90–91, **90–91**
    Mirren, Helen 91, **91**
    Presley, Elvis **88–89**, 95, **95**
    using fame for good 136–137, **136–137**
    see also Movies
Adams, Daniel Lucius "Doc" 117, **117**
Adenla (Yoruba crown) 27, **27**
The Adventures of Esplandián (Rodríguez de Montalvo) 73
Æthelstan, King (England) 13, **13**
Afonso I (Afonso Henriques), King (Portugal) 12, **12**
African Americans
    Alexander, Claudia 161, **161**
    Alexander, Kwame 97, **97**
    Ali, Muhammad 126–127, **126–127**
    Bowen, Anthony 121, **121**
    civil rights movement 146–147, **146–147**
    Howard, Ayanna 143, **143**
    Hughes, Langston 97, **97**, 121
    Irving, Barrington 166, **166**
    James, LeBron **7**, 122, **122**
    King, B. B. 94, **94**, 95
    King, Martin Luther, Jr. 7, **7**, **146**, 147
    Lawrence, Jacob 102, **102**
    Leonard, "Sugar" Ray 115, **115**
    Marshall, Thurgood 121
    Obama, Barack 91, 147, **147**
    Persson, Markus "Notch" 92, **92**
    Poitier, Sidney 106, **106**
    Smith, Will 136, **136**
    Thomas, Vivien 152, **152**
    Williams, Daniel Hale 145, **145**
Agamemnon (legendary king) 82, **82**
Aging 142
Aguinaldo, Emilio 58, 59
Akbar the Great, Mogul emperor 55, **55**
Alaric I (Visigoth) 37, **37**
Aldrin, Edwin "Buzz," Jr. 158
Alexander, Claudia 161, **161**
Alexander, Kwame 97, **97**
Alexander the Great 53
Ali, Muhammad 126–127, **126–127**
Amazons 31, **31**
American Indians 14, **14**, 85, **85**
American Revolution 62
Amun-Ra (god) 77, **77**
Anamorphosis 103, **103**
Andronicus IV, Byzantine Emperor 57
Animal armor 66, **66–67**
Anker, Conrad 125
Annan, Kofi 132, **132**

Anne Boleyn, Queen (England) 25
Antarctica 167
Antoninus Pius, Emperor (Rome) 54
Anu (god) 70
Apollo missions **148–149**, 158–159, **158–159**
Apple Computer Company 154, 155
Aragorn (legendary king) **4**, 74, **74**
Archaeology 31, 80, 156, **156**
Architecture 100–101, **100–101**
Aristotle 135
Armor 66–67, **66–67**
Armstrong, Neil 158
Arsūf, Battle of (1191) **28–29**, 29
The Art of War (Sun) 38–39, **38–39**
Artabanus (Xerxes' adviser) 52
Arthur (legendary king) 79
Artists (painters) 102–103, **102–103**
Arts, kings of 88–107
Ashoka the Terrible, Emperor (India) 36–37, **36–37**
Ashurbanipal, King (Assyria) 70
Astronauts **5**, 139, 148, **148–149**, 158–159, **158–159**
Astronomers 150–151, **150–151**, 160–161, **160–161**
Athletes see Sports
Attenborough, David 163, **163**
Audubon, John James 162, **162**
Augustus II, King (Poland) 57
Authors 96–97, **96–97**
Auto racing 123, **123**
Aztec Empire 27, **27**, 67, **67**

B

Babylon 10–11, **10–11**, 87
Ballard, Robert 157, **157**
Barbier, Charles 140–141
Barnard, Christiaan 144, **144**
Barnard, Marius 144
Baseball 110–111, **110–111**, 117
Basketball **7**, 116, **116**, 122, **122**
Battle preparations 36–37, **36–37**
Baumgartner, Felix 166, **166**
Baylor, Elgin 121
Bean, Alan L. 158
Beowulf 83, **83**
Betrayed kings 52–53, **52–53**
Biking 167, **167**
Biles, Simone 123, **123**
Bingham, Hiram 156–157, **156–157**
Biodiversity 167
The Bionic Woman (TV show) 143
Birds of America (Audubon) 162
Bismarck, Otto von 63
Black Panther (superhero) **68–69**, 69, 75, **75**
Blalock, Alfred 152, **152**
Blind people 140–141
Blues music 94, **94**
Bolívar, Simón 7, **7**, 60–61, **60–61**
Bolivia: independence 61
Bolt, Usain 123, **123**
Bonaparte, Joseph 56
Bonaparte, Napoleon 36, 56, 60, 61, 62, 140

Books 96–97, **96–97**
Boseman, Chadwick 69, **69**, 75, **75**
Bowen, Anthony 121, **121**
Boxing 115, **115**, 126–127, **126–127**
Boyega, John 112, **112**
Boyes, Steve 167, **167**
Braille 141, **141**
Braille, Louis 140, **140**–141
Brazil: Pedro II 65, **65**
Britain see England
Broadway 90–91
Brokkr (mythological figure) 86
Brutus (Caesar's friend) 53, **53**
Bush, George H. W. 123
Bush, George W. 127, **127**
Byzantine Empire 33, 57, **57**

C

Caesar, Julius 17, 43, 53, **53**
Caesar Augustus 17, **17**
Calafia (legendary empress) 73, **73**
Calculus 151
California (mythical island) 73, **73**
Caligula, Emperor (Rome) 52, **52**
Camp, Walter 117, **117**
Camp David Accords 133
Canada, Vikings in 33
Cantacuzenus, Co-Emperor (Byzantine Empire) 57
Car racing 123, **123**
Carter, Howard 156, **156**
Carter, Jimmy 27, 133, **133**
Carthage 13, **13**, 47
Cartwright, Alexander 117
Cash, Johnny 97
Castles 46–47, **46–47**
Catapults 47, **47**
Catherine of Aragon, Queen (England) 25
Catherine the Great, Empress (Russia) 43, **43**
Celebrities, using fame for good 136–137, **136–137**
Cena, John 137, **137**
Cernan, Eugene A. **5**, 148, **148–149**, 159
Chan, Jackie 136–137, **136–137**
Change, kings of 128–147
Chaplin, Charlie 107, **107**
Charlemagne, Holy Roman Emperor 22, **22**, 78, 79, **79**
Charles IX, King (Sweden) 36
Charles XII, King (Sweden) 57
Cheese rolling 118, **118**
Chernow, Ron 91
Children's literature 96–97, **96–97**
Chin, Jimmy **5**, 108–109, 125, **125**
China
    The Art of War (Sun) 38–39, **38–39**
    Confucius 134, **134**
    Dong Zhiming 165, **165**
    Huangdi 73, **73**
    Liu Xiaobo 132, **132**
    Nu Gua (goddess) 83, **83**
    Qin Shi Huang Di 22, **22**
    rebel princes *vs.* Jingdi 43, **43**
    Sun Wukong (Monkey King) 84, **84**
    Yu the Great 82, **82**

Christian IV, King (Denmark and Norway) **26–27**

Christian X, King (Denmark) 64, **64**

Civil rights movement 146–147, **146–147**

Clay, Cassius *see* Ali, Muhammad

Cleopatra, Queen (Egypt) 17

Cleveland, Grover 56–57, **56–57**

Cnut the Great (Viking) 33, **33**

Code of Hammurabi 11, **11**

Colombia: independence 61

Columbus, Christopher 61

Comeback kings 56–57, **56–57**

Comic books 75, 98–99, **98–99**

Computers

    Apple Computer Company 154, 155

    composing music 142

    games 92–93, **92–93**

    miniaturization 152

    modeling 143

    3D printing 138–139, **138–139**

    voice computing 143

Concentration camps 64, 133

Confucius 134, **134**

Conrad, Charles "Pete" 158

Cook, James 19

Coppola, Francis Ford 104

Cornish, James 145

Cortés, Hernán 73

Cotton, Dorothy 147, **147**

Coyote (Native American trickster) 85, **85**

Crassus, Marcus Licinius 43, **43**

Creativity, kings of 88–107

Crenellations **46–47**, 47

Crete 80–81, **80–81**

Cronus (Titan) 76

The Crossover (Alexander) 97, **97**

Crowns 26–27, **26–27**

Crusades **28–29**, 29, 34, 35

Cuba: Spanish-American War 59

Cubism 102

Curie, Marie 153, **153**

Curie, Pierre 153, **153**

Cusco 20–21

Cyrus the Great, Emperor (Persia) 23, **23**

Czech Republic: bear-filled moat 46

D

Dahl, Roald 105

Dankaran-Tuman, King (Manden) 23

Darius I, King (Persia) 52

Darwin, Charles 153, **153**, 162

Dayu (Yu the Great) 82, **82**

De Grey, Aubrey 142, **142**

Defeated kings 62–63, **62–63**

Deganawida (Onondaga spiritual leader) 14

Denmark

    Beowulf 83, **83**

    Christian IV's crown **26–27**

    Christian X 64, **64**

    Cnut the Great 33, **33**

    World War II 64

Dido of Carthage (goddess queen) 13, **13**

Dingiswayo (Mthethwa ruler) 40

Dinosaurs 164–165, **164–165**

Disney, Walt 107, **107**

DJ Jazzy Jeff 136

Doctors 144–145, **144–145**, 152–153, **152–153**

Dong Zhiming 165, **165**

Dr. Seuss 96, **96**

Duke, Charles Moss, Jr. 159

Durendal (legendary sword) 78, **78**

E

Earle, Sylvia 131, **131**

Easter Island 72, **72**

Edward I, King (England) 16

Edward VI, King (England) 25

Egypt, ancient

    Amun-Ra (god) 77, **77**

    archaeology 156, **156**

    Cleopatra 17

    Narmer 13, **13**

    Tefnakht 37

    Tutankhamun 77, 156, **156**

Eiríksdóttir, Freydís 33, **33**

Elam 11

Eleanor, Queen (England) 35

Elephants, war 66, **66–67**

Elizabeth I, Queen (England) 25

Elizabeth II, Queen (United Kingdom) 63, **63**, 91

Empire builders 8–27

England

    Æthelstan 13, **13**

    Cnut the Great 33, **33**

    colonies 62, 63

    Elizabeth II 63, **63**, 91

    George III 62, **62**

    Henry VIII **1**, 2, 7, 25, **25**

    Industrial Revolution 120–121

    Mary II 51, **51**

    Richard I (the Lionheart) **4**, **28–29**, 29, 34, 35, **35**

    Richard II 42, **42**

    Shakespeare, William 53, 91

    William I (the Conqueror) **16**, 16–17

    William III **4**, 50–51, **50–51**

    World War I 63

Enheduanna (priestess) 71

Enkidu (legendary wild man) 70–71

Environmentalists 130–131, **130–131**, 162–163, **162–163**

The Epic of Gilgamesh 70–71

Eric Bloodaxe (Viking) 32, **32**

Erik the Red (Viking) 33

Ethiopia: Haile Selassie I **6**, 45, **45**

Europa (mythological figure) 80

Evans, Sir Arthur 80

Evolution 153

Exploration

    Age of Exploration 58, **58**

    books 73

    Columbus, Christopher 61

    Easter Island 72

    extreme adventurers 166–167, **166–167**

    ocean 131, **131**, 157

    research and discovery 156–157, **156–157**

F

Ferdinand I, King (Naples and Sicily) 56, **56**

Ferdinand VII, King (Spain) 61

Ferrer, José 106, **106**

Flamsteed, John 151

Football 117

Forests 130–131, **130–131**, 163

Forkbeard, Sweyn 33

Fortresses 46–47, **46–47**

Fossils **164**, 164–165

Founding figures 72–73, **72–73**

France

    Hundred Years' War 42

    Louis XIV 51

    Louis XVI 53, 56, 62, **62**

    Marie Antoinette 53, **53**, 62

    Napoleon I 36, 56, 60, 61, 62, 140

    World War I 63

Franz Ferdinand, Archduke (Austro-Hungarian Empire) 63

French Revolution 53, 56, 60, 62

Freydís Eiríksdóttir 33, **33**

Futurists 142–143, **142–143**

G

Gajah Mada 15, **15**

Gaming pioneers 92–93, **92–93**

Gatehouses 46, **46**

Gehrig, Lou 111

Gehry, Frank **100**, 100–101

Geisel, Theodor Seuss 96, **96**

Genghis Khan, Emperor (Mongolia) **4**, 7, 30–31, **30–31**

George III, King (England) 62, **62**

Germany

    Wilhelm II 63, **63**

    World War I 63

    World War II 64, 164

Gessius Florus (Roman governor of Israel) 42

Gilgamesh (god-king of Sumeria) 70–71, **70–71**

Gladiators *vs.* Crassus 43, **43**

Gods and goddesses

    Amun-Ra 77, **77**

    gadgets 86–87, **86–87**

    Gilgamesh 70–71, **70–71**

    Indra 77, **77**

    Ishtar 71, **71**

    Nu Gua 83, **83**

    Odin 76–77, **76–77**

    Zeus 76, **76**, 80, 87

Goro Nyudo Masamune 78

Gravity 150, 151

Great Britain *see* England

Greece, ancient 52, 53, 135, **135**

Greek mythology

    Agamemnon 82, **82**

    Amazons 31, **31**

    Hades's helmet 87, **87**

    Minos 80–81, **80–81**

    Zeus 76, **76**, 80, 87

Guardians of the Galaxy (movies) 112, **112**

Guidotti, Galgano 79

Gustav II Adolf, King (Sweden) 36, **36**
Gymnastics 123, **123**

H

Haakon the Good 32
Hades (god) 87, **87**
Hadid, Zaha 101, **101**
Hadrian, Emperor (Rome) 54
Haile Selassie I, Emperor (Ethiopia) **6**, 45, **45**
Haise, Fred 159, **159**
Hamilton (musical) 91, **91**
Hammurabi, King (Babylon) 7, 10–11, **10–11**
Han dynasty 43, **43**
Hannibal of Carthage 47
Harald Hardrada, King (Norway) 33, **33**
Haring, Keith 103, **103**
Harold Godwinson, Earl 16–17
Harrison, Benjamin 57
Harry Potter books 119
Hawaii 18–19, **18–19**
Heart surgery 144–145, **144–145**, 152
Helbing, Dirk 143, **143**
Helen of Troy 82
Helm of Hades 87, **87**
Henry II, King (England) 35
Henry VIII, King (England) 1, 2, 7, 25, **25**
Hero Twins (legendary Maya kings) 72, **72**
Hewlett, William 155
Hiawatha 14, **14**
Himiko, Queen (Japan) 23, **23**
Hinduism 55, 77
Hitler, Adolf 64
Hockey, underwater 118, **118**
Hōjō Tokimune, Emperor (Japan) 44, **44**
Honjo Masamune (legendary sword) 78, **78**
Honnold, Alex 124, **124**, 125
Hooke, Robert 151
Hotu Matu'a (legendary king of Easter Island) 72
Howard, Ayanna 143, **143**
Huangdi (legendary emperor of China) 73, **73**
Hughes, Langston 97, **97**, 121
Hull, Charles **5**, **138**, 138–139
Hunahpu (legendary Maya king) 72, **72**
Hundred Years' War 42
Hungary: Stephen I 12, **12**, 27, **27**
Hydrothermal vents 157
Hypatia (mathematician) 151, **151**

I

Ibrahim, Nizar 164, **164**
In the Heights (musical) 90–91, **91**
Inca Empire **8–9**, 20–21, **20–21**, 156–157
India
    Akbar the Great 55, **55**
    Ashoka the Terrible 36–37, **36–37**
    independence 63
    Indra 77, **77**
    Payeng, Jadav 130–131, **130–131**
    Shah Jahan 16, **16**
    war elephants 66, **66–67**
Indiana Jones movie series 104, 105, 157
Indonesia: Gajah Mada 15, **15**
Indra (god) 77, **77**
Industrial Revolution 120–121

Iran: Kiani Crown 27, **27**
Iroquois Confederacy 14
Irving, Barrington 166, **166**
Irwin, James B. 159
Isabella I, Queen (Spain) 61, **61**
Ishtar (goddess) 71, **71**
Islam
    Abu Bakr 24, **24**
    Akbar the Great 55, **55**
    Muhammad 24
    Saladin **28–29**, 29, 34, **34**, 35
Israel 42
Italy
    Ferdinand I 56, **56**
    World War II 45
Ívarr the Boneless (Viking) 32, **32**

J

Jaguar warriors 67, **67**
Jahangir, Mogul Emperor 16
James, LeBron **7**, 122, **122**
James II, King (England) 51
Jane Seymour, Queen (England) 25
Japan
    Himiko 23, **23**
    Hōjō Tokimune 44, **44**
    Jingu 79
    Kumagusu, Minakata 163, **163**
    Miyazaki, Hayao 107, **107**
    Oda Nobunaga 17, **17**
    samurai armor 67, **67**
    swords 78, **78**, 79, **79**
    World War II 59, 78
Jayanagara, King (Majapahit Empire) 15
Jerusalem 34, 35, 42
Jews 42, 64, 133
Jingdi, Emperor (China) 43, **43**
Jingu (legendary empress of Japan) 79
Jobs, Steve 93, **129**, 154, 155, **155**
John V Palaeologus, Byzantine Emperor 57, **57**
John VII, Byzantine Emperor 57
Johnson, Dwayne 113, **113**
Johnson, Philip 101
Joyeuse (legendary sword) 79, **79**

K

Kalakaua, King (Hawaii) 19
Kalaniʻōpuʻu, King (Hawaii) 19
Kamehameha, King (Hawaii) 18–19, **18–19**
Kaplan, Matt 81
Keller, Helen 140, 141, **141**
Kiani Crown 27, **27**
Kilby, Jack 152, **152**
King, B. B. 94, **94**, 95
King, Martin Luther, Jr. 7, **7**, **146**, 147
Kings
    characteristics 168–169
    introduction 7
Kiwalaʻo 19
Knossos (ancient city) 80–81, **80–81**
Knowledge kings 148–167
Kościuszko, Tadeusz 43
Krak des Chevaliers, Syria 47
Kublai Khan 44
Kumagusu, Minakata 163, **163**
Kurzweil, Raymond 142, **142**

Kusama, Yayoi 103, **103**
Kush, kingdom of 37, **37**
Kuti (general) 15

L

Land mines 133
Langeni 40–41
Lawrence, Jacob 102, **102**
Lawrence, Jennifer 113, **113**
Laws: Code of Hammurabi 11, **11**
Lawson, Jerry 93, **93**
Leadership 168–169, **168–169**
Leakey, Louis 157, **157**
Leakey, Mary 157
Lee, Bruce 114, **114**
Legends, lords of 68–87
Leibniz, Gottfried 151
Leif Erikson 33
Lenin, Vladimir 63
Leno, Jay **139**
Leo III, Pope 22
Leonard, Bernadette 115
Leonard, Roger 115
Leonard, "Sugar" Ray 115, **115**
Lepidus, Marcus 17
Lewis, John 147, **147**
Libecki, Mike 167, **167**
Liliuokalani, Queen (Hawaii) 19, **19**
Lion Capital of Ashoka (sculpture) 37, **37**
Liston, Sonny **126–127**, 127
Literature 96–97, **96–97**
Liu Xiaobo 132, **132**
Loki (Norse trickster god) 86
The Lord of the Rings (Tolkien) **4**, 74, **74**
Louis XIV, King (France) 51
Louis XVI, King (France) 53, 56, 62, **62**
Lovell, Jim 159, **159**
Lucas, George 104, **104**, 105

M

Maathai, Wangari 163, **163**
Macapagal, Diosdado 59
Macedon: Philip II 53, **53**
Machu Picchu, Peru **8–9**, 20, 21, **21**, 156–157
Magar, Rajesh 167, **167**
Majapahit Empire 15, **15**
Majuli, India 130–131
Malaysia: Gajah Mada 15, **15**
Mali: Sundiata Keita 23, **23**
Maps
    Age of Exploration 58
    Mongol Empire 31
Marcus Aurelius, Emperor (Rome) 54, **54**
Marie Antoinette, Queen (France) 53, **53**, 62
Mark Antony 17
Marshall, Barry 153, **153**
Marshall, Thurgood 121
Martial arts 114, **114**, 136–137
Mary, Queen (England) 25
Mary II, Queen (England) 51, **51**
Masamune, Goro Nyudo 78
Mathematics 150–151
Maya 72, **72**
Medicine 144–145, **144–145**, 152–153, **152–153**

Meier, Sid 93, **93**
Menelik II, Emperor (Ethiopia) 45
Mercians 13
Merlin, Joseph **116**, 116–117
Mesopotamia
    Gilgamesh 70–71, **70–71**
    Hammurabi 7, 10–11, **10–11**
    Ishtar 71, **71**
Messi, Lionel 122, **122**
Mexico
    Aztec Empire 27, **27**, 67, **67**
    Maya 72, **72**
Michael IV, Byzantine Emperor 33
Military masterminds 28–47
Minecraft (game) 92
Minos (legendary king of Crete) 80–81,
    80–81
Minotaur 80–81, **81**
Miranda, Lin-Manuel **5**, 90–91, **90–91**
Mirren, Helen 91, **91**
Mitchell, Ed 158
Mitchell, Jackie 111, **111**
Miyazaki, Hayao 107, **107**
Mjölnir (Thor's hammer) 86, **86–87**
Moai (giant statues) 72, **72**
Moats 46, **46**
Moctezuma II, Emperor (Aztec) 27, **27**
Mogul Empire 16, **16**, 55, **55**
Mongolia
    Genghis Khan **4**, 7, 30–31, **30–31**
    Kublai Khan 44
Monkey King (Sun Wukong) 84, **84**
Moon **5**, 72, **148–149**, 158–159, **158–159**
Mountain biking 167, **167**
Moussallam, Yves 166, **166**
Movies
    action heroes 112–114, **112–114**
    Black Panther **68–69**, 69, 75, **75**
    celebrities using fame for good
        136–137, **136–137**
    monarchs 104–105, **104–105**
    Oscars 106–107, **106–107**
    see also Actors
Muhammad (prophet) 24
Muir, John 162, **162**
Mumtaz Mahal, Mogul empress 16
Muramasa Sengo 78
Muramasas (legendary swords) 78
Music and musicians
    King, B. B. 94, **94**, 95
    Miranda, Lin-Manuel **5**, 90–91, **90–91**
    Presley, Elvis **88–89**, 95, **95**
    Silverstein, Shel **96**, 96–97
    Smith, Will 136, **136**
Musical theater 90–91, **91**
Muslims *see* Islam
Mussolini, Benito 45
Mutapa (African empire) 75

N

Naismith, James 116, **116**
Nandi, Princess 40, 41
Naples: Ferdinand I 56, **56**
Napoleon I, Emperor (France) 36, 56, 60,
    61, 62, 140
Narmer (Egyptian pharaoh) 13, **13**
Native Americans 14, **14**, 85, **85**

Nazis 64
Newman, Paul 137, **137**
Newton, Isaac **150**, 150–151
Nicholas Romanov II, Tsar (Russia) 63, **63**
Ninurta (rain god) 87
Nobel Peace Prize 132–133, **132–133**, 163
Norse mythology 76–77, **76–77**, 86, **86**
Northumbria: Eric Bloodaxe 32, **32**
Norway
    Christian IV's crown **26–27**
    Cnut the Great 33, **33**
    Eric Bloodaxe 32, **32**
    Harald Hardrada 33, **33**
Noyce, Robert 152, **152**
Nu Gua (snake goddess) 83, **83**
Nūr al-Dīn (Muslim ruler) 34
Nur Jahan, Mogul empress 16

O

Ō-yoroi (samurai armor) 67, **67**
Obama, Barack 91, 147, **147**
Oberon (king of the faeries) 83, **83**
Ocean exploration 131, **131**, 157
Ocēlōtl (Aztec warriors) 67, **67**
Octavian, Emperor (Rome) 17, **17**
Oda Nobuhide 17
Oda Nobunaga 17, **17**
Odin (god) 76–77, **76–77**
Okavango Delta, Botswana 167
Olaf II Haraldsson, King (Norway) 33
Olympic Games 115, 122, 123, **123**, 127, **127**
Oscars (Academy Awards) 106–107,
    106–107
Ozturk, Renan 125

P

Pachacuti Inca Yupanqui **8–9**, 20–21,
    20–21
Painters 102–103, **102–103**
Pajitnov, Alexey 92, **92**
Paleoanthropology 157
Paleontology 164–165, **164–165**
Pausanias (bodyguard) 53
Payeng, Jadav 130–131, **130–131**
Peasant uprisings 42, **42**, 43
Pedro II, Emperor (Brazil) 65, **65**
Pepin the Short, King (Franks) 22
Persia
    armor 67, **67**
    Cyrus the Great 23, **23**
    Xerxes I 52, **52**
Persson, Markus "Notch" 92, **92**
Peru
    independence 61
    Machu Picchu **8–9**, 20, 21, **21**, 156–157
    Pachacuti Inca Yupanqui **8–9**, 20–21,
        20–21
Petty, Richard 123, **123**
Pharaohs *see* Egypt, ancient
Philip II, King (Macedon) 53, **53**
Philip II, King (Spain) 58
Philip the Bold, King (France) 79
Philippines: revolution **48–49**, 49, 58–59,
    58–59
Philosophers 134–135, **134–135**
Photography 125
Physics 150–151

Picasso, Pablo 102, **102**
Piye, King (Kush) 37, **37**
Plate armor 67, **67**
Poetry 96–97, **96–97**
Poitier, Sidney 106, **106**
Poland: Stanislaw I 57, **57**
Pompey the Great 43
Portal (game) 93
Portugal: Afonso I 12, **12**
Poseidon (god) 80, 87
Pratt, Chris 112, **112**
Presidents of the United States
    Bush, George H. W. 123
    Bush, George W. 127, **127**
    Carter, Jimmy 27, 133, **133**
    Cleveland, Grover 56–57, **56–57**
    Obama, Barack 91, 147, **147**
    Roosevelt, Theodore 162
    Truman, Harry **59**
Presley, Elvis **88–89**, 95, **95**
Prosthetics 138–139, **139**
Prussia: Wilhelm II 63, **63**

Q

Qin Shi Huang Di, Emperor (China) 22, **22**
Quantum Conundrum (game) 93
Quidditch 119, **119**

R

Rap music 136, **136**
Rapa Nui (Easter Island) 72, **72**
Rasputin 63
Reddy, Raj 143, **143**
Remus 73, **73**
Revolutionary War (U.S.A.) 62
Rhea (Titan) 76
Richard I (the Lionheart), King (England)
    4, **28–29**, 29, 34, 35, **35**
Richard II, King (England) 42, **42**
Rim-Sin, King (Larsa) 11
Robinson, Cleveland 147, **147**
Robotics 143, **143**
Rock-and-roll music **88–89**, 95, **95**
Rock climbing **5**, 124–125, **124–125**
Rodríguez, Simón 60
Rodríguez de Montalvo, Garci 73
Roland (warrior) 78
Roller-skating 116–117, **117**
Roman Empire
    Alaric I and 37
    Caesar, Julius 17, 43, 53, **53**
    Caligula 52, **52**
    gladiators *vs.* Crassus 43, **43**
    Marcus Aurelius 54, **54**
    Octavian 17, **17**
    Zealots *vs.* Vespasian 42, **42**
Rome (city) 73
Romulus 73, **73**
Roosevelt, Theodore 162
Roxas, Manuel **59**
Running 123, **123**
Russia
    Catherine the Great 43, **43**
    Nicholas Romanov II 63, **63**
    World War I 63
Rustin, Bayard 147, **147**
Ruth, Babe 110–111, **110–111**

S

Sagan, Carl **160**, 160–161
Saladin (Muslim army leader) **28–29**, 29, 34, **34**, 35
Salish people 85
Samurai armor 67, **67**
Scale armor 67, **67**
Schmitt, Harrison "Jack" 159
Schwarzenegger, Arnold 113, **113**
Scientists 148–167
Scott, David 159
Scott, George C. 107, **107**
Scythians 31, **31**
Self-made monarchs 12–13, **12–13**
Senzangakhona, King (Zulu) 40
Sepak takraw 119, **119**
Seuss, Dr. 96, **96**
Seven-branched sword 79, **79**
Shah Jahan, Mogul emperor 16, **16**
Shaka, King (Zulu) 40–41, **40–41**
Shakespeare, William 53, 91
Sharur (mythical mace) 87, **87**
Shepard, Alan 158
Shuster, Joe **98**, 99
Sicily: Ferdinand I 56, **56**
Sid Meier's Civilization (game franchise) 93, **93**
Siege weapons 47, **47**
Siegel, Jerry **98**, 99
Sigismund III, King (Sweden and Poland) 36
Silverstein, Shel **96**, 96–97
Sin-Muballit, King (Babylon) 10
Sindri (mythological figure) 86
Skydiving 166
Slavery 65, 121
Smith, Jada Pinkett 136
Smith, Will 136, **136**
Soccer 122, **122**
Socrates 135, **135**
Space 139, **158–159**, 158–161
Spain
    Isabella I 61, **61**
    Napoleon's invasion 61
    Philippine Revolution **48–49**, 49, 58–59, **58–59**
    South American colonies 60–61
Spanish-American War 59
Spartacus (Roman slave) 43
Spielberg, Steven 104, 105, **105**
Spinosaurus 164, **164**
Sports 108–127
    action movies 112–114, **112–114**
    baseball 110–111, **110–111**, 117
    basketball **7**, 116, **116**, 122, **122**
    behind-the-scenes kings 116–117, **116–117**
    boxing 115, **115**, 126–127, **126–127**
    Olympic Games 115, 122, 123, **123**, 127, **127**
    superstars 122–123, **122–123**
    up-and-coming sports 118–119, **118–119**
    YMCA 116, 120–121, **121**
Staircases, in castles 47, **47**
Stanislaw I, King (Poland) 57, **57**

Star Wars (movies) 104, 112, **112**
Stephen I, King (Hungary) 12, **12**, 27, **27**
Stewart, Martha 137
Stromer, Ernst 164
Sullivan, Anne 141
Sumeria: Gilgamesh 70–71, **70–71**
Sun Tzu 38–39, **38–39**
Sun Wukong (Monkey King) 84, **84**
Sundiata Keita, Emperor (Mali) 23, **23**
Superman 98–99, **98–99**
Supernatural rascals 84–85, **84–85**
Sweden
    Beowulf 83, **83**
    Charles XII 57
    Gustav II Adolf 36, **36**
    Viking wall hanging 77
    World War II 64
Sweyn Forkbeard (Viking) 33
Swift, Kim 93, **93**
Swigert, Jack 159, **159**
Swords, legendary 78–79, **78–79**
Syria
    castles 47
    Saladin **28–29**, 29, 34, **34**, 35

T

T'Challa, (legendary king) **68–69**, 69, 75, **75**
Tefnakht (Egyptian pharaoh) 37
Telescopes 151, **151**
Teresa de León, Countess (Portugal) 12
Tetris (game) 92
Theseus (mythological figure) 81
Thomas, Vivien 152, **152**
Thor (god) 86, **86**
3D printing 138–139, **138–139**
Titanic, R.M.S. 157
Tolkien, J. R. R. 74
Track-and-field events 123, **123**
Trebuchets 47, **47**
Trojan War 82
Truman, Harry **59**
Tunisia: Dido of Carthage 13, **13**
Tutankhamun (Egyptian pharaoh) 77, 156, **156**
Tyler, Wat 42, **42**

U

Underwater hockey 118, **118**
United Kingdom *see* England
United Nations 132
United States
    American Revolution 62
    control of Philippines 59
    see also Presidents of the United States; *specific people*

V

Varini, Felice 103, **103**
Vasarhelyi, Elizabeth Chai 125
Vedic religion 77
Venezuela: independence 61
Verus Augustus, Lucius Aurelius, Emperor (Rome) 54
Vespasian (Roman general) 42, **42**
Video games 92–93, **92–93**
Vikings 32–33, **32–33**, 77

Viracocha Inca 20
Visigoths 37, **37**
Volcanologists 166, **166**

W

Wakanda (legendary kingdom) **68–69**, 69, 75, **75**
Wallace, Alfred Russel 153, **153**
Walls, castle **46–47**, 47
War elephants 66, **66–67**
War strategy 38–39, **38–39**, 41, **41**
Warren, Robbin 153, **153**
Wiesel, Elie 133, **133**
Wilhelm II, Emperor (Germany) and King (Prussia) 63, **63**
William I (the Conqueror), King (England) **16**, 16–17
William II, King (Netherlands) 50
William III (of Orange), King (England) **4**, 50–51, **50–51**
Williams, Daniel Hale 145, **145**
Williams, George 120, 120–121
Williams, Jody 133, **133**
World War I 63, 153
World War II
    bombings 164
    concentration camps 64, 133
    Denmark 64
    Ethiopia 45
    Holy Crown of Hungary 27, **27**
    Japan 59, 78
    Philippines 59, **59**
    war artists 102, **102**
Wozniak, Steve 93, 154, **154**, 155
Writers 96–97, **96–97**
Wukong (Monkey King) 84, **84**

X

Xbalanque (legendary Maya king) 72, **72**
Xerxes I, King (Persia) 52, **52**

Y

YMCA 116, 120–121, **121**
Yoruba crown 27, **27**
Yosemite National Park, California, U.S.A 108–109, 124, 162
Yoshimoto, Imagawa 17
Young, John 159
Young Men's Christian Association (YMCA) 116, 120–121, **121**
Yu the Great (legendary emperor of China) 82, **82**

Z

Zealots 42
Zeus (god) 76, **76**, 80, 87
Zhou Yafu (general) 43
Zorbing 119, **119**
Zulu 40–41, **40–41**

FOR LUCIUS AND LACHLAN:
Little today, leaders tomorrow —C. M.

FOR THE KIDS READING THIS NOW:
You are the kings and queens of the future.
May you always rule with wisdom. —S. W. D.

Since 1888, the National Geographic Society has funded more than 12,000 research, exploration,
and preservation projects around the world. The Society receives funds from National Geographic Partners, LLC,
funded in part by your purchase. A portion of the proceeds from this book supports this vital work.
To learn more, visit natgeo.com/info.

NATIONAL GEOGRAPHIC and Yellow Border Design are trademarks of
the National Geographic Society, used under license.

For more information, visit nationalgeographic.com,
call 1-800-647-5463, or write to the following address:
National Geographic Partners
1145 17th Street N.W.
Washington, D.C. 20036-4688 U.S.A.

Visit us online at nationalgeographic.com/books

For librarians and teachers: ngchildrensbooks.org

More for kids from National Geographic: natgeokids.com

National Geographic Kids magazine inspires children to explore their world with fun yet educational articles
on animals, science, nature, and more. Using fresh storytelling and amazing photography,
Nat Geo Kids shows kids ages 6 to 14 the fascinating truth about the world—
and why they should care. **kids.nationalgeographic.com/subscribe**

For information about special discounts for bulk purchases,
please contact National Geographic Books Special Sales: specialsales@natgeo.com

For rights or permissions inquiries,
please contact National Geographic Books Subsidiary Rights: bookrights@natgeo.com

Designed by Ashita Sawhney, Ashita.Design

The publisher would like to thank the following people for making this book possible: Kate Hale, executive editor;
Jen Agresta, project editor; Sanjida Rashid, art director; Lori Epstein, director of photography;
Liz Seramur, photo editor; Sarah Wassner Flynn, contributing writer; Ariane Szu-Tu, editor; Paige Towler and
Kathryn Williams, associate editors; Avery Naughton, editorial assistant; Scott Vehstedt, fact-checker; Maya
Meyers, editorial consultant; Alix Inchausti and Molly Reid, production editors; and Anne LeongSon and Gus Tello,
production designers.

For their review of selected content, special thanks to Oren Falk, associate professor of history and medieval
studies, Cornell University; Kevin C. MacDonald Ph.D. FSA, professor of African archaeology, University College
London Institute of Archaeology; Adrienne Mayor, research scholar, classics and history and philosophy of
science at Stanford University; Laura Miller, Ph.D., Eiichi Shibusawa-Seigo Arai Endowed Professor of Japanese
Studies and professor of history, University of Missouri–St. Louis; Dr. Jennifer Houser Wegner, associate curator,
Museum of Archaeology and Anthropology, University of Pennsylvania; Dan SaSuWeh Jones; and Dr. Herman Viola.

Hardcover ISBN: 978-1-4263-3533-4
Reinforced library binding ISBN: 978-1-4263-3534-1

Printed in Hong Kong
19/PPHK/1